50+ AND LOOKING FOR
∞ LOVE ∞
ONLINE

50+ AND LOOKING FOR

LOVE

ONLINE

BARBARA HARRISON

THE CROSSING PRESS
FREEDOM, CALIFORNIA

Excerpts from *Origins of Architectural Pleasure* by Grant Hildebrand, reprinted by permission of the publisher, University of California Press. Copyright ©1999 The Regents of the University of California.

For information on bulk purchases or group discounts for this and other Crossing Press titles, please contact our Sales Manager at 800/777-1048.

Visit our website on the Internet: **www.crossingpress.com**

Library of Congress Cataloging-in-Publication Data
ISBN 1-58091-042-4

∞ WITH LOVE TO ∞

Tania Grossinger, a steadfast friend through all these crazy days,
and
Josh & Jill Silverman, the nicest people in New York,
and
LSS, because

ACKNOWLEDGMENTS

My sincere thanks to the hundreds of men and women who so generously shared their time, their stories, their advice, and their most private thoughts with me. I learned something about the kindness of strangers during the writing of this book—strangers who answered question after question after question and then cheerfully invited me back for more, if more information was needed. And it often was!

For help way above and beyond, my thanks also to Cindy Harvey and Brad Schepp of AOL; Bill Schreiner, Executive Director of Love@AOL; Nancy Fedder, Personal Ads Manager of *New York Magazine*; John Randell, Assistant Classified Advertising Manager of *Washingtonian Magazine*, and Cindy Conrad, Classified Advertising Manager of *Washingtonian Magazine*.

Lastly, my warmest appreciation to my agent, Claire Gerus, who helped shape and pull this project together, and did it with a smile.

Thank you, thank you, thank you, one and all.

∞ TABLE OF CONTENTS ∞

Introduction

There was a time when crossing the 50+ threshold meant the best part of life was behind us. My, how times have changed. Today 50+ is more a beginning than an end and it means whatever we want it to mean. To Stephanie Simms, an ebullient Florida entrepreneur, it means "I'm happy with myself now. My life is for laughing, loving, and living." To Chris Ryan, a retired aerospace engineer in Ireland, it means, "I'm old enough to know about lots of things that are silly to do, but young enough to enjoy doing them." To Beau Billeaudeaux, a day trader in Washington State, it means "We've been through it all and now we have the freedom to do what, where, and when we damn well please."

It's true. The good news is we're living longer, better, healthier than ever before. We're wiser about the ways of the world. We're tuned in, we're clued in, we're comfortable with ourselves. We're free to *be* ourselves. Released from carpool duty and PTA and Little League, we're finally the stars of our own lives.

If there's a downside, it's that too many of us are alone. There are more than 18,000,000 singles aged 50+ in the U.S., and whether we're divorced or widowed or among the never-married, we share the desire for love. But no matter how much we might wish for love, finding it is easier said than done. Some of us are held back by our memories, some by uncertainty. Most of us are held back by fear, because whoever we are and wherever we live, we all face the same obstacle: dating.

The comedian Garry Shandling has said he's afraid of three things: bungee jumping, roller coasters, and dating. Like roller coasters and bungee jumping, dating is a plunge into the void. It's scary enough at 30; at 50+ it can be absolutely spooky. Where do we meet people? How do we meet people? If we do meet someone, the getting-to-know-you rituals can run the gamut from awkward to humiliating. And the competition! At 50+, how do we measure up to competition that is often younger and (wrongly) thought to be sexier than we are? How do we deal with it?

The Personals offer solutions to these problems. Why the Personals? Let's start by looking at some numbers. Last year, more than a million Personal ads were placed in newspapers, magazines, newsletters, and professional journals nationwide, drawing tens of millions of responses. A publication like *New York Magazine*, the premier venue for Personal ads in New York City, draws as many as 8,000 responses every week.

Numbers on the Internet are even more dazzling. For example, Love@AOL boasts 200,000 photo Personals in its database and draws 1,000 new ads a day. Two million four hundred thousand people enter the site every month. Or consider AOL's Digital City Personals, with a whopping 52,000,000 page views monthly.

Depending on the publication and the web site, 50+ers account for anywhere from 11 percent to 50 percent of all Personal ads, and these numbers, like the others, keep growing. To quote an old gambling maxim: "You have to go where the action is." For 50+ singles, the action is in the Personals.

Time is all there is, so make the most of it. Let the Personals help you make these 50+ years the *best* years of your life.

CHAPTER 1

NINE QUESTIONS TO HELP YOU FIGURE OUT WHO YOU ARE NOW

WHETHER YOU DECIDE TO PLACE YOUR PERSONAL ad on the Internet or in newspapers, magazines, or newsletters, you have to begin by asking yourself who you are now. If you honestly believe you already know who you are and what you want, please skip to page 42.

We can see the physical changes that have happened over time. Look in the mirror and there they are, staring back at us. A glance in the mirror is like taking inventory—is that a wrinkle or a laugh line? Is my hair a little thinner on top? Is my skin a little dry? Do I need a brighter shade of lipstick? Have I put on a few pounds? These are the externals we deal with every day. They're the outer wrappings, far easier to assess than what's *inside* the package.

The way we think, the way we feel, our desires, our doubts, our fears, our dreams are true measures of who we are. It's tempting to claim that these measures are unchanged, that we're the same people we were years ago, but are we? Sorry, the answer is no. We may be more so or less so, we may be better about some things than we used to be and worse about others, but we're definitely not the same. Does it matter? Yes, it does, because before we can know what we want now, we have to know who we *are* now.

Call it a journey of self-discovery. If that's too fancy, call it a personal update. Use the nine questions below to do some exploring. Drag out all the old assumptions and give them a good shake. Look into those secret places of heart and mind. Be honest and, above all, relax. There are no right or wrong responses. There's no failing grade for this quiz. So find a comfortable chair, settle back, and ask yourself: 9 key questions.

∞ What Is Your Philosophy of Life? ∞

A philosophy of life can be described as the attitude you bring to life, the mindset that governs your thoughts and choices. You may not want someone who thinks exactly the way you do, but you should want someone who views life in the same way. Imagine a photo of a deserted street and the lights of an unknown city beyond. If you show the photo around, some people will see adventure, some will see danger, and some will merely see a deserted street and the lights of an unknown city. What would you see?

Are you adventurous? Stephanie Simms would no doubt see adventure, but that wasn't always true. After a disastrous marriage and an even more disastrous divorce, she withdrew emotionally, gained a lot of weight, and generally let herself go. "I did everything I could to keep men away," she explains. "It was just too painful. But that was then. That was before the Personals totally changed my life." Now a happy, confident, slimmed-down and tummy-tucked Stephanie espouses a philosophy that matches her life. "Work like you don't need the money, love like you've never been hurt before, dance like no one is watching." It's a wonderful philosophy, and if it strikes a chord in you, then you should be looking for someone open, someone uninhibited, someone who knows how to love and *be* loved.

Are you practical? If your philosophy is somewhat less romantic, something along the lines of "Love many, trust few, learn to paddle your own canoe," your soul mate is probably the sensible, straightforward type.

Are you cynical? If you believe it's best to "get what you can get while you can get it," you want someone hard-edged and clear-eyed about life. No dreamers or poets need apply.

Are you an optimist? Beau Billeaudeaux has perhaps the best philosophy for 50+ers: "We're younger than we'll ever be again, so live life to the fullest." My own philosophy is one I share with Chuckles the Clown of the old *Mary Tyler Moore Show*: "A little song, a little dance, a little seltzer down your pants." Meaning, don't take yourself too seriously. Meaning, life is short, enjoy it.

2

∞ WHAT IS YOUR BIGGEST FEAR? ∞

Everybody has fears. At 50+ these fears are likely to center around things like health and money and loneliness. There may be fears about adult children who are going through bad times. Or there may be fears about grandchildren who are sinking into trouble. There are fears that come with retirement. There's the real, if unfounded, fear that time has passed you by. What are your fears? Which one is uppermost in your mind?

Loneliness often translates into neediness. Don't let it, because neediness turns people off. Peter Brent, 57, a thoughtful, articulate New York architect, sums up the attitude of a lot of men when he says he would like women "to take more responsibility for their own emotional well-being." Susan Smith, 51, a New York real estate broker, echoes a lot of women when she says, "I want a man who stands on his own two feet." The fact is, at 50+ most people want a relationship of equals. "Like for like," concurs Joanie Yellin of California. "I had that kind of relationship once. It's the only kind of relationship I want now."

If your fear concerns family, look for someone who's family-oriented and sympathetic to family problems. Some 50+ers feel they've already paid their dues; they've reared their children, sometimes in complicated, blended families; they've looked after elderly parents, and now they're done with all that. If you're not, look elsewhere.

If your big *fear is money,* first determine whether you have real cause to worry or whether you're scaring yourself for no good reason. If your finances are indeed shaky, avoid ads looking for someone "financially secure." No matter how perfectly you seem to match up in other areas, it won't work. Money is a classic point of conflict, especially at 50+. Don't doom a relationship before it even begins. Don't waste your time.

Examine your own fears. They're part of who you are and they're part of what you'll take along with you when you meet someone new. And be aware—the someone new will have fears, too.

3

∞ WHAT IS YOUR IDEA OF PERFECT LUXURY? ∞

Luxury is in the eye of the beholder. What would please you most?

- A vacation at an exclusive beach resort?

- Designer clothes?

- Dinner at a four-star restaurant?

- Flying first class?

- A top-of-the-line set of golf clubs?

These are luxuries that everybody's thought about from time to time. Maybe one of them is on your wish list, maybe not.

Or maybe one of these is on your wish list:

- A day all to yourself; no errands, no chores, no decisions to make, no phone calls, nobody knocking at the door—a day completely without responsibilities?

- Being pampered at a spa; massage, facial, body wrap, the works?

- A whole day with your grandchild, at the zoo, at the museum, hiking in the woods, sailing, fishing?

If you're the exclusive beach resort type, you might not be happy with someone who prefers lazy days at home, gardening or reading. If you see yourself in designer clothes at four-star restaurants, can you also see yourself baiting fish hooks and hoisting sails? Think about it. How *do* you see yourself?

4

⟨⟩ WHO ARE YOUR HEROES? ⟨⟩

Heroes have taken a beating in this tabloid age of ours, but there are still people you can respect and admire for the way they live their lives or do their work or somehow make the world a better place. A hero could be someone you know, or someone you simply know about. It could be a family member, a teacher who inspired your child, a volunteer at a community center, a member of the clergy who truly lives his or her faith. It could be a public figure: a writer, artist, or performer. Scandals and soap operas aside, it could even be a politician or an athlete. Of all the possibilities, whom do you admire most?

- Someone idealistic and self-effacing, like a Mother Teresa?

- Someone rich and arrogant, like a Donald Trump?

- Someone creative?

- Someone compassionate?

Realize that the qualities you admire are the same qualities you *value*. And what you value in life says a great deal about who you are.

5

∞ Do You Like Surprises? ∞

Surprises come in all shapes and sizes. There are the small, snappy ones—unexpected calls, letters bringing unexpected news. There are the big, startling ones: a chance encounter with an old love, an unexpected business proposition, an unexpected call from the doctor's office, that can transform your life. There's no telling what surprises are waiting just around the corner. If you welcome them, you welcome spontaneous moments. If you don't, you appreciate the orderly and uneventful. Ask yourself: are you a maker of lists, a taker of notes, a keeper of scores, or are you a free spirit who goes with the flow?

- Can you find a happy medium between the two?

- Are you willing to compromise? How flexible are you?

- Can a list maker find happiness with a free spirit?

- Conversely, can a free spirit find happiness with a list maker?

The answer to the last two questions is yes: a free spirit can find happiness with a list maker and a list maker can find happiness with a free spirit—if both people are willing to bend a little.

Life without structure is messy, while life with too much structure is boring. If you're flexible enough to agree that there's more than one way to do things, you're flexible enough to accept change in your life. Change is good. Keeps the juices bubbling!

6

∞ How Important Is Religion to You? ∞

Is religion in the forefront of your life?

- Is it something you turn to only in times of crisis?

- Is it something you rarely think about but something that's part of you, quietly guiding your attitudes and choices?

- Have you drifted away from your religious roots and do you want to return to them?

- Are you searching for spiritual values outside the context of organized religion?

Do you define yourself as a believer?

- Can you describe your religious beliefs?

- Are you tolerant of religious beliefs that differ from yours?

- Do you try to persuade others to adopt your beliefs?

- Could you comfortably share a life with someone who doesn't share your beliefs?

Do you define yourself as a non-believer?

- How tolerant are you of other people's religious beliefs?

- Do you try to persuade others to abandon their religious beliefs?

- Are you hostile to religion or merely indifferent?

Religion can be a bond between people or a source of discord. If compatibility is the key to a happy relationship, religion is an important key to compatibility. Don't underestimate it and don't be dishonest about it.

∞ ARE YOU A SPENDER OR A SAVER? ∞

At 50+, money issues take on a special importance. It's a time to reassess needs and expectations, to take a long, hard look at the present and a longer, harder look at the future. Ask yourself:

- Are you naturally thrifty?

- Do you like to splurge now and then?

- Are you where you want to be financially?

- What are your financial goals for retirement?

- On a scale of 1–10, how much financial risk are you willing to take?

Big risk-takers and big spenders are always going to be at odds with the cautious and the thrifty. Decide where your comfort zone is and stay in it. Keep it in mind when you meet someone new. If you don't, you might spend the rest of your life arguing about the Visa bill!

∞ DO YOU CRAVE EXCITEMENT OR SERENITY? ∞

First of all, remember that this isn't necessarily an either/or. You can enjoy the serenity of a walk in the woods and also get a kick out of testing the odds in Las Vegas. You can love the unpredictability of your life but still want a degree of consistency in the actions and reactions of a soul mate. Not everything has to be logical, romance least of all. Just figure out your basic preference and go on from there.

Serenity calls for someone centered and accepting. Excitement calls for someone who likes to live it up. Are you able to take a little something from column A and a little something from column B?

What is your idea of excitement?

- A spur of the moment trip?

- Hot air ballooning?

- An X-rated video?

What is your idea of serenity?

- A drive in the country?

- A twilight stroll on the beach?

- The feeling that you've met all of life's challenges and now you just want to relax?

How willing are you to try something new? Don't be too quick to reject someone whose life is less—or more—active than yours. Serenity can lead to complacency if it's not spiced with a dash of excitement now and then. Excitement can turn into chaos without moments of serenity to calm the soul. Can the twain meet? Yes!

9

∞ WHAT WAS YOUR HAPPIEST TIME ? ∞

Here's yet another way men and women are different. Ask a man about the happiest time of his life and he's apt to recall events linked to sports, business, or sex. Ask a woman the same question and she's apt to recall her wedding day or the birth of her children or the years when her marriage and children were young. When a woman talks about the day she made partner, or got her broker's license or her masters degree, you hear a voice brimming with satisfaction and pride. But *happiness* is something else. For most women, happiness is something that touches the heart. For most men, let's face it, happiness is something that touches the testosterone level.

Men and women can't expect to remember happiness in the same ways, but the remembering itself is what counts. What do you remember?

- What made you happy in the past?

- Who made you happiest?

- What distinguishes these memories? What makes them special?

- Are there parallels between happy times then and happy times now?

In the opinion of Ann Sayre, a writer who lives on Cape Cod, "Happiness at 50+ is saner but deeper. We know what life has been, and we know what we want it to be now. For me, 50+ is like starting over, but with a much, much better sense of who I am."

Anyone who has lived 50+ years has experienced great highs, great lows, and a gazillion variations in-between. We are who we are because of these experiences. So think about them and chart your journey from then to now. The *now* is what's important. A clear-cut sense of self is not only liberating, it's a big confidence builder.

There is a theory that good things happen to people who expect good things to happen. That's an oversimplification, but it's true that good things are more likely to happen to people who are receptive to good things. This is more than positive thinking. It's positive *energy*. Put positive energy to work for you.

Chapter 2

What Kind of Person Are You Looking For?

DON'T MAKE THE SAME MISTAKES TWICE. AT 50+ our tastes are set, right? We know what makes someone sexy, right? We know what our type is, right? Right. But only up to a point. If you make hard and fast rules about what is or isn't for you, you limit your opportunities. Even worse, you could be falling into a trap.

It's important to remember that being drawn to the same type over and over again is sometimes nothing more than being drawn to the familiar. The strong, silent type that was your college ideal still attracts you today. Your ex was blue-eyed and charming, and blue-eyed charmers still melt your heart today. Ask yourself whether it's chemistry or just the pull of memory.

If it's chemistry, consider changing the formula. If it's memory, make sure you're not leaving anything out, like the fact that the strong, silent one didn't know the first thing about how to communicate and didn't care. Or the fact that the ex's blue eyes roamed often and far. Don't let the memory of love lead you into the kind of situation that caused you grief before. And for heaven's sake, don't let memory hold you back.

Joan Safir, 55, is a realtor who lives in upstate New York. "I loved my life," she says. "I loved being married." But after 28 years of marriage her husband left her for a younger woman. Joan ran a Personal ad seeking—and describing—a man who could have been her husband's twin, right down to details such as his height and the length of his hair. Not surprisingly, every man she met through her ad was a disappointment. Again, not surprisingly, she swore off Personal ads altogether. More than a year after her divorce she isn't dating anyone or going out very much. She admits she is "alone and lonely."

There are several morals to this unhappy story. One is that you can't let yourself get stuck in the past. Another is that if you *are* stuck in the past, you have to acknowledge it and fight your way out.

The Personals aren't magic. They won't heal all the hurts or turn back the clock. What they will do, if you use them properly, is give you a chance at a fresh start. Take the chance. Here are some words of wisdom spotted on a sign at a subway token booth in Manhattan: "If you always do what you've always done, you'll always be what you've always been."

Give a lot of thought to your interests and hobbies. In the past you may have shared many interests with your partner. Those interests may have become your interests, if only by default. But things may be different now. You may be playing more golf and less tennis or vice versa. You may be more of a moviegoer than you used to be. You may recently have taken up a new hobby or gotten into computers.

Any interest or hobby you're serious about, anything that takes a lot of your time, should be mentioned in your ad or in your reply to someone else's ad. If you're an avid traveler, chess player, exerciser, say so. If you love to go bowling or dancing or bird watching—and would miss it if you had to give it up—say so. A new relationship shouldn't deprive you of something you truly enjoy, and it won't if you're honest from the start.

Here's an example: This man's ad stresses his serious interest in music by placing it first. "Opera Lover, widowed white male, 62, 6'1" and 230 lbs., loves music and the arts, seeks trim, intelligent woman, 50–58, with similar interests, for companionship plus." The ad is clear and direct, a winner!

John West doesn't expect to share everything with the woman he meets, but wants to share his major interest—the outdoors—and said so in his ad. "Outdoorsman, 52, 6'2", 210 lbs., enjoys tennis, bicycling, gardening, sailing, anything outdoors. Conservative values, liberal attitude. Seeking an attractive woman who enjoys the outdoors, is happy with life, loves herself and could love another." This is an excellent ad, no unnecessary frills. What you see is what you get.

However you choose to spend your leisure time, you have to decide how much of it you want to share with someone else. Ask yourself whether you're a "togetherness" person or an "I need my space" person? This is another compatibility issue. A "togetherness" person is likely to feel excluded by an "I need my space" person. An "I need my space person" is likely to feel smothered by a "togetherness" person. Either way there will be arguments and hurt feelings, so figure it out sooner rather than later.

Will Simon, a 63-year-old accountant in California, says, "I used to think that the only difference between men and women was the plumbing, but I've come to realize that men and women really *are* different. There's nothing left to do but enjoy the differences."

Yes, but some differences are more problematical than others. One of the songs from the score of *My Fair Lady* poses an interesting (and politically incorrect) question: "Why can't a woman be more like a man?" I paraphrased this question many times to many different men—asking them to describe the ways they wished women would be more like men in dealing with relationships.

Chris Ryan, the retired aerospace engineer, said he liked things the way they were, summing up his feelings with a jaunty "Vivé la difference." But virtually everyone else zeroed in on the way women communicate.

- Peter Brent, the New York architect, said, "I wish women would be more direct about what they are thinking and feeling. It's hard to always have to look for subtle clues."

- Jim Greene, a Washington journalist, said he wished women "would be more honest about what they're thinking."

- John West said, "Honesty and openness are top priorities in a woman. She should say what's on her mind."

- Stan Hewes, 60, a systems manager from Connecticut, asked, "Why can't women be more up front? It's no fun trying to guess what they mean."

Ironic, isn't it? While women complain that men don't share their feelings often enough, men complain that women don't express their feelings clearly enough. If you're 50+ and looking for love you have to learn to communicate your feelings.

Men, open up a little. Be honest about who you are now. Be honest about how you want to spend the rest of your life.

Women, be more direct. Who are you now and what do you really want?

Men and women, if you have trouble translating thoughts into words, practice. Invest in an inexpensive tape recorder and use it to explore your thoughts. Try describing yourself, your interests, and your hopes for the future. Keep talking about yourself until it feels comfortable. Put the tapes away for a couple of days and then play them back. You may be surprised by what you hear—you may learn some interesting things about yourself.

It's never too late. No one is ever too old for a healthy dose of self-knowledge.

CHAPTER 3

WHAT KIND OF RELATIONSHIP DO YOU WANT?

AMBIVELENCE IS AN ONGOING PROBLEM FOR SOME PEOPLE: ambivalence. Scott Hart is a 53-year-old psychotherapist who has been using the Personals on the Internet. "I like to think I want a committed relationship, but since I've never been married, perhaps I don't really want to marry. I'm aware that there is a difference between the stories I tell myself and what I am really willing to commit to."

Scott's experiences with the Personals haven't clarified anything for him. "I've been having an e-mail correspondence with a woman whose husband left her after thirty years of marriage. I think, for her, it's more a matter of wanting to make contact again. Regain herself. Heal herself. She has her own mourning to deal with. Many women after divorces are just testing the waters."

True. Many of the recently divorced or widowed aren't ready for new relationships. Joan Safir, the woman whose husband left her for a younger woman, is a perfect example of this. Despite all evidence to the contrary, she's still hoping her husband will come back to her. At least for now, there's no room for another relationship or another man in her life.

Jane Nelson, 62, a commercial real estate broker in Queens, New York, offers yet another example. "I had quite a few responses from my Personal ad on the Internet. One of the men I went out with was extremely witty and imaginative. I had a great time. We both did. So I was really looking forward to the next date. My mistake. The second date might have been entertaining, except that he brought his dead wife Betty along. His conversation all night was 'Betty used to say' or 'Betty used to think' or 'Betty used to wear.' I couldn't wait for the evening to end. Needless to say, I never saw him again."

There's another kind of ambivalence lurking in the problem of the "rebound person." Stephanie Simms, the ebullient Floridian whose life was changed by the Personals, talks about transitions. "After a divorce or a breakup, there are people who want a new relationship but not *the* relationship. They just need someone to get their emotions from one place to another. That someone is the rebound person. It may not be deliberate. Not everyone knows what's going on in their minds, or what their needs really are. But deliberate or not, it's unfair. It's something to look out for. Nobody wants to be the rebound person. It's a can't-win situation because in the end, the rebound person gets dumped."

The lesson here is obvious. If you have to take the past with you when you meet someone new, you're not *ready* to meet someone new. Think about it. Ask yourself: Are you in transition, needing to connect again but not quite ready to commit? To be suddenly single again, whether through death or divorce, is to be hurt and confused. Not to mention angry and distracted. So what's next for you? If you could design the perfect scenario for yourself, what would it be?

This is another place where a tape recorder comes in handy. Talk about your former spouse, explore your feelings. Talk about what you want for yourself now. Be honest, don't censor yourself. Keep talking until you get it all out. It's liberating to say exactly what's on your mind. And if you don't know exactly what's on your mind, this is a great way to get at the truth. Put the tapes away and play them back a couple of days later. Listen carefully to what you hear. If the truth hurts, that's okay; it'll only hurt for a little while.

The following questions are for anyone considering writing a Personal ad—and especially for the ambivalent singles among us. What's right for you?

- Are you looking for love?

- Are you looking for a long-term relationship?

- Are you looking for marriage?

- Are you looking for companionship with no formal commitments?

- Are you just looking for dates?

"Dates," says Carly Berg, a 60-year-old Texan. "I've been married twice. That's enough. I've been divorced for eight years now. I have no desire to get married again, but I'm not a hermit. I like going out. I like enjoying myself. The Personals give me a large dating pool so I can make my own choices, no strings attached."

Holly Lloyd, a Manhattan-based writer, is another woman who isn't interested in remarrying, but who wants something more than casual dates. "I'm comfortable being on my own. I travel a lot and I like being free to go off whenever I want without having to match up with someone else's schedule. I'm not interested in dating around either. I'm looking for companionship. I want to share my life with one man, but without lifetime commitments on either side."

Also on the subject of companionship, there's Jackie Boyer, 58, a Houston businesswoman. "I had an ad in a Houston newspaper and received a letter from a man named David. We wrote back and forth a few times and then agreed to meet for breakfast. I wasn't real attracted to him when we first met, but he was very nice so I agreed to go out with him again. We had a lovely time. We got along so well. He's kind and sweet, and a very loving person. We've been together a year. I am crazy about him and he loves me too. We still have our separate houses. I doubt we will ever marry—he had a bad marriage and is not keen on doing it again. But he is wonderful, a wonderful companion and friend. Just let the ladies and the guys know there is hope for all of us."

Hope comes with many different labels, of course. Far more typical of expectations in the Personals is Karen Hicks, a divorced New Yorker who wanted to marry again. "My first three ads flopped," she recalls. "I got responses, but from men who were all wrong for me. On my fourth try, I added the words 'serious relationship' and added the word 'stable' in describing myself. I met my husband through this ad. He said it was the 'serious relationship' part that caught his eye. He didn't want to be going out on dates for the rest of his life. He wanted a serious relationship with someone stable."

You are the only person who knows what you truly want. You are the only person who can make it happen for yourself. So do it. Remember that there are people out there who are just as anxious as you are to connect with someone. Give them a chance to find you!

CHAPTER 4

WHERE AND WHEN SHOULD YOU PLACE YOUR PERSONAL AD?

PERSONAL ADS CAN BE TRACED BACK TO THE DAYS of the old West, where lonely pioneer men depended on them to bring mail-order brides to the isolation of vast, unsettled lands. There are no more pioneers, no more lands to settle, but loneliness is as much a part of the human condition now as ever it was. If social and romantic connections were hard to make on the frontier, they are just as hard to make in modern cities and towns. Perhaps harder for those of us who are 50+.

The quandary is neatly summed up by John West. "Every year that goes by, you lose the ability to meet people. You don't do the things you did when you were young—you don't go out drinking or partying, and you probably don't meet new people at work. Every year that goes by is a net loss."

The Personals offer a lively solution to the problem, but remember that *where* you place your ad is as important as what your ad says. It's simple: the wrong choice will waste time, money, and hope; the right choice will increase your chances of success. Choices are what the Personals are all about.

- You get to choose what to reveal about yourself.

- You get to choose the responses you like.

- You get to choose the people you want to contact.

- You get to choose the people you want to see.

∞ Where to Place Your Personal Ad ∞

The first choice you have to make—the one that will affect all the others—is where to place your ad. Today, the possibilities are nearly endless. Newspapers? Magazines? Professional journals? Newsletters? The Internet? Think about the best venue or venues for your particular needs. Luck won't put you in the right place at the right time; it takes planning. You know what you want. Now find the quickest way to get there.

Newspapers

For starters, do your homework. Buy all the newspapers in your area and study their Personal ad sections. Note the kind of people each section draws. Note the kind of ads. Do you like what you see? Would you feel comfortable there? Make special note of the sections in which 50+ men and women are well represented. Those are the ones for you, because those are the ones that will be read by other 50+ers. Don't waste your time on sections that cater to a younger demographic unless you are in search of a younger demographic. If you are, be sure to choose a Personal ad section that is hospitable to this mix. You don't want to be the only 50+er on the page in search of a 30+er.

City Magazines

For city dwellers, publications like *Washingtonian Magazine, Los Angeles Magazine*, and *New York Magazine* are prime venues for Personal ads. They are likely to be more expensive than the

Personals in your local newspapers, but they are also likely to deliver a more motivated and responsive readership.

New York Magazine, for example, charges $37 per line with a two-line minimum, but draws as many as 8,000 responses each week. Check out the cost and the rate of response for the magazines in your area. How do the figures compare to the figures for your local newspapers?

Don't base you choice *solely* on costs. Ask yourself where your ad will have the best chance. Remember that your Personal is an investment in your future. If you look at it that way, you might want to expand your opportunities by trying a combination approach—placing ads in both a newspaper and a magazine. See which of the two venues yields the most promising results. Trial and error is part of the process in the beginning.

Newsletters

Carve out a niche for yourself. Newspapers, magazines, and the Internet offer the most direct access to the widest possible audience, but don't underestimate the value of newsletters. Use them to reach other 50+ singles who share your interest in whatever. The environment? Poetry? Elvis? *Any* mutual interest is an advantage. It's a ready-made topic of conversation that can help ease you through the first telephone call or the first meeting. Something as simple as a shared interest can help ease you into a new relationship, so don't leave this stone unturned. Pay a visit to your local library for a directory of newsletters published in the United States.

Religious Publications

For many people, religion creates the strongest bond of all. If you share this feeling, investigate the Christian, Jewish, or other religious weeklies and monthlies published in your area. Remember that honesty is the only policy for Personal ads in these publications. Born again means born again. Orthodox means orthodox. Don't try to fake it.

Your church or synagogue or other place of worship may publish a monthly bulletin featuring upcoming events and news of the congregation. Some of these bulletins may include listings of singles looking for companionship or for more serious relationships. If so, be sure to add your own listing to the group. If not, suggest that the bulletin add a "Friendship" or "Introductions" page. What better way to meet someone who shares your faith and your values?

The Internet

Last, but certainly not least, there's the Internet. Rule One is to use it efficiently. If you're an experienced Net surfer you know where everything is. If you're new to cyberspace, spend some time getting your bearings.

You can access Personal ads by age group, by state, by city, by religion. They can also be accessed in more specialized newsgroups—for example: the tall, the fat, the kinky, etc. Personal profiles can be accessed via Internet chat rooms. (Not sure how to access these sites? See the next chapter.)

Explore the sites that interest you, read the ads, and see

where you feel at home. If you're not yet online, you probably have a friend who is, and who will let you borrow an e-mail address. Don't overlook this option because you "hate computers." Hate them or love them, they're here to stay and they touch on all aspects of modern life, including the Personals.

Trish McDermott, executive manager of the online service Match.com, says, "Online dating exposes you to thousands of people from around the country who are interested in your profile. But you have to pick your spots. There are certain places you would never walk into. The Internet parallels that. You have to pick the right Internet environment."

Fans of Print Personals

- Ann Sayre says, "I like the slower pace of print Personals. I like the idea of someone actually taking the time to write a letter, stamp it, and mail it, instead of just dashing off something on the computer. E-mail's quick, but what's the hurry? Half the fun of meeting a new man is getting to know him. Getting to know the possibilities. Anticipation can be very sexy.

- Karen Hicks says, "You can tell a lot about a man by the kind of letter he writes. E-mail isn't the same."

- Jim Greene says, "I've been pleasantly surprised by the quality of the responses and the women I've met through the print Personals. Print is better focused than the Net. Not as wide open."

- Nancy Fedder, Personal Ads Manager of *New York Magazine*, says, "If you're new to the Personals, you might want to start with print ads. With the Net, there's no paper trail. Anybody can tell you anything and it can take quite a while to get the truth."

Fans of Internet Personals

- Phyllis Robbins, 53, of New York, says, "I have had very good experiences with the Internet. It's non-threatening and secure if you do it right. I pick sites that make everyone put in a bio before they can browse. With a bio you can see who you're dealing with before you answer."

- Bill Schreiner, Executive Director of Love@AOL, says, "What makes online dating successful is the marriage of the new technology and the time-honored tradition of letter writing. E-mail gives you a way to choose your moments. It's positive reinforcement and instant gratification. Online ads are efficient. You can do a search specific to your needs. You get unlimited space for your bio. And If you aren't ready for face-to-face relationships, you can start communicating online while you build your confidence."

- Scott Hart says, "The advantage of online ads is that you always get e-mail responses. That's a positive, good feeling. When you're feeling lonely, someone's there. When you don't feel like going out, there are people to communicate with."

- Julie Reyes says, "I love hearing that happy computer voice say, 'You've got mail.' It makes my day."

There's truth in all these comments. Online ads cast a wider net.

Is wider always better? Not always, not if it draws geographically undesirable responses. Print ads take more effort but draw more focused responses. Does this give them an edge over the Net? Not necessarily, not if the print publications in your area reach too small a readership.

So take your cue from successful investment managers and diversify. Many publications are now putting their Personal ads on their Web sites as well. If your local publications haven't started doing this, then plan to do it yourself. Choose the print ad sites that are appropriate for you and the online sites you're comfortable with, and get ready to attack on all fronts. All's fair in love, if not in war.

Whatever print or Internet environment you choose, remember that timing is everything. Before you place an ad or start composing responses, take a look at the calendar. If the holidays are approaching and you're going to be busy with family, forget the Personals until the holidays are over. If you're planning a trip out of town in the next couple of months, forget about the Personals until you return. If the grandchildren are coming to visit, wait until they've gone back home. In other words, clear the decks. Set aside time that's just for you and put your own interests first. You've spent years doing things for other people— do this for yourself.

Don't let the wrong reasons dictate the timing of your ad. What are the wrong reasons? Here's a brief sampling:

- Because you need a date for an upcoming event

- Because you need a date for New Year's Eve

- Because summer is coming

- Because your (fill in the blank) birthday is coming

- Because your ex just remarried

No need to list the right reasons—you know what they are. Keep them in mind every step of the way. Stay focused!

CHAPTER 5

MOVING AROUND ON
THE INTERNET

IF YOU'RE NEW TO THE NET, DON'T WORRY. ACCESS-
ing online Personals is easy even for computerphobics.

If you have the Web address of a specific Personal ads site
(for example, www.match.com), simply type it into the address
box on your screen and press Enter. If you don't have an address,
or are looking for addresses of other sites offered by your
Internet provider, use the keyword box, usually located at the
top of your screen. Move your cursor to the keyword box and
type in the keyword "Romance." This keyword will link you to
Personal sites as well as to certain chat rooms.

The keyword "Romance" works with all Internet providers.
On AOL it will take you to Love@AOL, where the photo
Personals are grouped by sex, age, geographic location, and race.
It will take you to the Christian photo Personals site and the
Jewish photo Personals site, both grouped by sex, age, and geo-
graphical location.

It will also take you to Digital City, a local-content network
with a Personals site grouped by geographic location, as well as

lists of restaurants, movies, and events in each location. Here's a typical search, step by step:

- Type in keyword Romance

- Click on Christian Singles (or Jewish Singles)

- Click on Women Seeking Men, or Men Seeking Women

- Click on By Age

- Click on By State

- Read the headlines

- See a headline you like? Click on it, read the whole ad, look at the photo

- E-mail your response to the e-mail address in the ad

- Take a break and wait to see if you get a response

- If you do get a response, and you like it, keep going

Note #1: Web addresses for Personal ads can be found in the Appendix.

    Note #2: Most Internet providers recommend that you create a separate screen name for Personal ads e-mailing. To create another name, follow the prompts (instructions) on your screen.

∞ CHAT ROOMS ∞

Chatting online is one of the Internet's most popular features. Here's how you enter a chat room:

- Type the keyword Chat Rooms in the keyword box. It will take you to a chat room screen.

- Select a Chat Type, clicking either on chats created by your Internet provider or on chats created by the provider's members (the participants).

- Select a Chat Category—Romance, for example.

- Click on View Chats. The chats shown in the list box will change to those in your selected category.

- You can watch the conversation, which takes place in the middle of your screen. When you first enter a room, you'll see a message from the online host telling you which room you are in. A moment later, the conversation will start to scroll by. Every line shows the person's screen name.

- You can join the conversation. At the bottom of the screen is a box. To contribute a comment, simply type it in the box and click "Send." Your comment will appear in the conversation with your screen name in front of it. Everyone in the room will be able to see what you've typed.

- You can see who else is in the room. On the right side of the screen is a list of the people there. As they enter and leave, the names will appear and disappear from the screen.

- If you want to send a private message, or find out more about someone, or ignore messages from someone, double click on his or her name from the list on the right side of the screen.

- To create a private chat, first create a screen name for your chat and enter it in the Input box. Be sure to remember how you entered the name so that you can invite family and friends to join your chat. If someone has invited you to join his chat, be sure he gives you his name exactly as he entered it. Once you have typed in the name of the chat you want to create or join, click on "Go Chat" to begin chatting.

Note #1: Formats change, so be sure to follow the prompts on your screen.

Note #2: Follow your Internet provider's suggestions for protecting your privacy online.

Note #3: Don't limit yourself to Romance chat rooms. If you're interested in the stock market, try an Investment chat room. If you're interested in sports, try a Sports chat room, etc. You can easily access a wide range of topics from the list box or menu on your screen. Members of most chat rooms are encouraged to enter their profiles, which in turn can be accessed by going to the member's screen name and clicking on Profile. If the person is eligible and interesting, send an Instant Message. Never overlook an opportunity.

∞ LEARNING THE LANGUAGE ∞

To save space and/or money, Personal ads are filled with abbreviations. The most common ones include:

S	Single
M	Married
D	Divorced
SEP	Separated
NM	Never Married
G	Gay
BI	Bisexual
B	Black
W	White
A	Asian
H	Hispanic
C	Christian
J	Jewish
F	Female
M	Male

ISO	In Search Of
P	Professional
GU	Geographically Undesirable
NR	Non-Religious
NS	Non-Smoker
YO	Years Old
LTR	Long-Term Relationship

Chat Room Abbreviations

LOL	Laugh Out Loud
ROTF	Rolling On The Floor (laughing)
BTW	By The Way
RSN	Real Soon Now
IMHO	In My Humble Opinion
IMNSHO	In My Not So Humble Opinion
GMTA	Great Minds Think Alike
F2F	Face-To-Face
TTFN	Ta Ta For Now
AFK	Away From Keyboard

BRB	Be Right Back
IM	Instant Message

Chat Room Symbols (also called Emoticons or Smileys)

:)	Smile
;)	Wink
:D	Laughing
:(	Frown
:'(	Crying
>:-}	Is A Devil
O;-)	Is An Angel
}}	Hug
:*	Kiss
:X	My Lips Are Sealed
:P	Sticking Out My Tongue

Chapter 6

How to Write
Your Personal Ad

First impressions count, and never more than in the Personals. Your ad will succeed or fail based on what you have to say about yourself and how you say it. What positive qualities are people drawn to? A sense of humor is the one quality on everyone's list. In this context a sense of humor means the ability to laugh at yourself and at life's little absurdities, the ability to keep things in perspective. Nobody likes a sorehead.

Don't be negative in your ad. Concentrate on what you want, not on what you don't want. And follow the one basic guideline everybody agrees on: Don't lie. Lies will always catch up with you, count on it.

- *New York Magazine*'s Nancy Fedder adds that "the right frame of mind is important. Attitude can make a difference in the Personals. Everyone has something positive to accentuate in an ad—great smile, great skin, great legs, etc. If there's something about yourself you like, somebody else will like it too." She acknowledges that this point can be difficult

for some women. "Ask a woman about a physical characteristic and you can hold your breath till you pass out. Men answer right away. Women need to feel that same degree of
confidence."

- Phyllis Robbins says that, "The purpose of any ad is to get
  someone to respond and that's obviously true of the
  Personals. You need a catchy headline. You have to market
  yourself, and the same marketing principles that apply in
  business apply here. The more open and real you are, the
  more you will appeal to people. You need to write in a
  friendly style and to show you have a sense of humor. Make
  no mention of a past bad relationship or anything negative at
  all. If you are positive and upbeat, that's a go. A good photo
  will increase your chances by fifty percent."

- Peter Brent says, "A good ad conveys a sense of who you are
  as a person. You don't have to wear your heart on your sleeve,
  but there should be a sense of who you are on the inside as
  well as the outside."

- Love@AOL's Bill Schreiner suggests, "You should always
  personalize your Personal. For example, instead of saying, 'I
  like to read books,' describe the kind of books you like to
  read, or talk about a book you've read that touched you in
  some special way. Love is in the details."

- Jackie Boyer advises, "Make it a hard and fast rule to keep romance down to zero when you first start writing to each other."

Knowing who you are and what you want will make it easier for you to compose a successful Personal ad. Start by making a list,. What do you like best about yourself? What do your friends like best about you? Include everything and then narrow your list down to the four or five qualities that define you as an individual. Don't be modest. If, for example, you happen to be clever and caring and fun, say so. If you're intelligent and kind and have big blue eyes into the bargain, say so.

Each of us is our own unique blend of qualities and quirks. Don't be afraid to be who you are, and don't be afraid to say who you are.

Ineffective ads just lie on the page, taking up space. Don't make these mistakes:

> CLONE SOUGHT—highest quality man, 52, seeking twin in female form.

Comment: A silly ad. This man is much too pleased with himself. Give him a blonde wig and a mirror. Don't give him your phone number.

> ATTRACTIVE WIDOW, 58, seeks attractive gentleman, 50s–60s.

Comment: This ad is flat. It says nothing.

> SWM, 50s, seeking SWF, etc., etc., etc.

Comment: If this world-weary man doesn't have enough energy to write a real ad, he doesn't have enough energy to meet someone new.

> SEEKING A FRIEND or companion, 50s, someone tall, fair, trim, and feminine, with fine features, nice legs, who is refined, elegant, romantic, sweet, for this 50+ psychiatrist.

Comment: The writer of this ad has nothing to say about himself and has too many requirements for the woman he wants to meet. Are there issues of control here?

> I'LL KNOCK YOUR SOCKS OFF! Strikingly gorgeous, definitely sexy, professional DF, 50s, playfully funny, vivacious, passionate, spicy, great legs, desires man with great looks, humor, intelligence, heart, for out of this world romance.

Comment: This ad promises quite a lot. Fine, *if* everything is true. If not, expect to be very embarrassed.

> DO YOU FIT MY CRITERIA
> of a single man who en-
> joys the arts and intellec-
> tual conversation? If so,
> send your résumé to this
> similar, beautiful SWF, 52.

Comment: Another silly ad. Probably meant to be humorous, but just sounds pretentious. The lesson here is, when it comes to humor, don't try too hard.

> FIRST TIME AD, SF, 55,
> loves travel, tennis, ISO
> SM 52-62, for friendship
> and more.

Comment: Don't waste a headline—nobody cares if it's your first ad. And don't leave out the qualities and interests you're seeking in someone else.

> ATTORNEY, SWM, 52, seeks attractive, professional woman, 50s.

Comment: Another flat, boring ad that says nothing.

> BE MY DADDY. Beautiful sexy brunette with brains seeks a kind, financially secure man, 50+, to take care of my basic needs. Not looking for a serious relationship, but willing and able to satisfy your needs.

Comment: Make no mistake about it, ads of this kind are sex for money, and they're not kidding!

Effective ads leap off the page and grab your attention. Here in italics are some especially winning phrases:

I WANT IT ALL: friendship, romance, intimacy. Successful, happy, in shape male, 58, seeks a strong, attractive, slim, intelligent woman, 50s, *who has the capacity to give back what she gets.*

DENIM SHIRTS, ROLEX, suburban male, 59, 6', 173 lbs., balding, likes exercise, investing, dogs/cats, visuals, grandchildren, travel, great food, good books, fishing, beach. *Fluent in menopause.* Seeking smart, kind, affectionate *partner for life.*

ROMANTIC RENAIS-
SANCE man seeks sophisti-
cated, spiritual friend/lover.
My specs: Early 60s, 6',
divorced entrepreneur,
adventuresome, stable,
sensitive. Your specs:
50–65, pretty, street-
smart, open, cultured,
emotionally available.

A NICE GUY, divorced, early
50s, professional. I try to
balance doing well with
doing good. Enjoy lively
conversation and explor-
ing new places, nature,
family, friends, fires, films
with happy endings. ISO
compatible woman, 50s,
slim, fit, feminine, affectionate, adventurous,
non-snob. Extra credit if
skilled in massage and if fix-
ing healthy meals is a
favorite pastime, and/or do
standup comedy.

SMILES, PASSION, warmth, companionship, and loyalty. That's what I can promise you if you can reciprocate. WM, 57, seeks a woman, 50s, who can receive, return, and enjoy all of the above.

ADVENTUROUS, affectionate male, 55, well read, verbal, smart, and loving, seeking *a woman of wit and wisdom, for laughs, escapades, and forever.*

Gatherer needs hunter. SWF, 51, needs SWM, 50s, *who doesn't mind washing a dish once in a while* and who knows what this means: 'l-o-o-o-k at me.'

Healthy enough to be 30, smart to think 40, lucky to look 50, happy to tell you I'm 60. I seek one special guy who's always the romantic, kind and humorous too.

Dishy redhead with soft heart, entrepreneur, 53, mother of boys, 5 & 8, loves food, tennis, reading, music, art, travel. Seeks affectionate, accessible, *sensual BBQ partner with soul, purpose.*

A woman of substance, joyous, optimistic, very attractive, 50+, with *sexy sense of humor* and a passion for classical music, the outdoors, and Europe. *Wants to meet a man, 50+, with a generous spirit and a glint in his eye.* His children a plus.

Fabulous and fit, smart, pretty, successful professional woman, 52, with a great sense of humor, seeks a successful man in his 60s, *who has character, integrity, and laugh lines, to share the next 50 years (all right, 40 years).*

> My favorite men are listeners, 50–65, who know when or whether to speak; honest, inquisitive, *do-ers and be-ers*. I'm pretty, blue-eyed, red-haired, 60, with *depth, gentleness, warmth, wisdom, and passion.*

These are all excellent, well-thought out ads that illustrate several key points discussed earlier. The writers of these ads know who they are and what they want. They describe themselves with wit and originality, and they display a light touch. It's clear that they like themselves.

∞ THREE RULES FOR DESIGNING YOUR AD ∞

In the competitive world of the Personals, if you blend into the background you're lost. When you design your ad you may be designing your future, so put some pizzazz into it. Use your imagination and create a "designer original."

FIRST RULE: *Don't Be Generic, Be Specific*

Whatever you want to say, say it in your own unique voice. For example, in the 50+ Personals, everybody likes "dining out." B-o-r-i-n-g.

What kind of dining do you like?

- Cozy Saturday lunches before the movies?

- Dim sum and green tea for two?

- Intimate candlelight dinners, hold the violins?

- Pasta and Chianti?

- Low-cal gourmet adventures?

- Plain cooking and plain talk?

In the Personals everybody likes "long walks on the beach." Okay, but dress it up a little. Do you like...

- Long walks on deserted beaches?

- On the beach at midnight?

- At dawn?

- In autumn?

- After a storm?

Close your eyes and think about it. There you are on the beach...

- What kind of beach?

- What kind of day?

- What kind of night?

- Why are you smiling?

Second Rule: *Don't Be Bland*

In the 50+ Personals, everybody is "attractive." As a word, "attractive" doesn't say much. It can mean anything from "Well, at least I don't have two heads," to "Why, yes, that was my picture in *Vogue* last month." If you have to describe yourself as "attractive," pair it with something more descriptive—for example, "attractive honey blonde," or "attractive six-footer."

Consider such descriptive words as "Striking, Cute, Stylish, Beguiling, Distinguished-looking, Chic, Jaunty, Elegant, Lovely, Suave, Classic, Vivacious, Graceful, Sparkling, Dainty, Sleek, Charming, Polished Good Looks."

If you're lucky enough to be handsome or beautiful, a knock-out of either sex, don't be shy about it—say so.

THIRD RULE: *Don't Be Afraid to Add a Touch of Humor*

The New York man who described himself as "fluent in menopause" was rewarded with a mailbox full of replies. Find your own "fluency" and use it.

∽ QUALITIES MEN LOOK FOR IN WOMEN? ∽
∽ QUALITIES WOMEN LOOK FOR IN MEN? ∽

It's no secret that men and women are wired differently and have different ideas about what they want in the opposite sex.

MEN LOOK FOR:

- A woman who is willing to try new things

- A woman who is active and involved in life

- A woman who is warm and sensual

- A woman who has a young outlook

- A woman who is down-to-earth

- A woman who has an even temperament

- A woman who has an uncritical nature

- A woman who is affectionate

- A woman who likes to have fun

Karin Erikson, a counselor in Australia, sums up the female point of view in this wish list.

WOMEN LOOK FOR:

- A man who is honest, sincere, and communicative

- A loving, tender man who would respect me as I would respect him

- A man who would laugh with me

- A man who would be as affectionate as I am

- A man who would appreciate what I do for him, as I would love to spoil him

- A man who would remember also to spoil me

- A man who now and then would surprise me by arranging a romantic dinner

- A man who now and then would do something mad and crazy to show that he loved me

- A man who now and then would *tell* me he loved me, because it's wonderful to hear the words

Advice: Read these lists and think about them. But don't forget what you already know. Namely, that nobody gets everything they want. Namely, that real life always beats wishing. Always.

∞ KEY WORDS ∞

Here are some descriptive words that *both* men and women are drawn to:

active	loving
adventurous	loyal
affectionate	passionate
caring	romantic
compassionate	sensual
dynamic	sexy
faithful	sincere
financially secure	smart
financially independent	stable
fit	thoughtful
fun-loving	vigorous
funny	warm
healthy	warmhearted
kind	witty

Use the words that apply to you. Remember that many 50+ men and women are concerned about preserving assets for children and grandchildren; if you're financially secure, don't hesitate to say so.

Should you begin by describing what you look like? It's up to you. One of the advantages of being 50+ is that we're comfortable in our own skins. Not for us the soul-searching of 20+, the uncertain posturing of 30+. The difference is apparent in the Personals. A sampling of 30+ Personals turns up ads with such requirements as "beautiful young woman with 23" waist." Or "slim, up to 115 pounds." One ad placed by a "multimillionaire" listed thirteen separate requirements, eleven of them concerning physical appearance. What crust! Or as we say in New York, What *chutzpah*!

50+ Personals are less concerned with looks. That's not to say that looks don't matter. A trim figure, a sexy smile, sensational legs, are assets at any age—and if you've got 'em, flaunt 'em. But looks are only part of the picture. The best 50+ ads have insight and balance.

∞ SOME TOUCHY SUBJECTS ∞

WEIGHT

If you're carrying extra pounds, say so without apology. Men often list height and weight together. For women who choose not to be specific (and that's most of us), acceptable code words like "pleasantly round" or "full-figured" or "Rubenesque" get the point across. It's true that many men tend to favor slender women. But not *all* men. Bill Schreiner has the right take on it. "Since coming to Love@AOL, I've learned the larger lesson that there really is somebody for everybody."

HEIGHT

If you're a man under 5'8", list your height without apology. For example, "Trim 5'7", or "5'6" & Fit." It's true that many women tend to favor tall men. But not *all* women.

LOOK-ALIKES

Some of us think we look like movie stars. The advantage of saying so in an ad is that it conjures up instant mental images. The disadvantage is that it raises expectations. Spend time in front of a mirror before you compare yourself to a famous person. Do you really resemble that person or is there only a slight resemblance around the edges? Imagine meeting your date for the first time and seeing the look of disappointment in his or her eyes. Don't put yourself in an awkward position.

Modesty

Don't confuse sincerity with excessive modesty. The woman who described herself in her ad as "mildly intelligent" and the man who described himself as "okay for my age, 64," need to re-think their attitudes about themselves. Don't describe yourself or the person you are seeking in anything but positive terms. Be confident and welcoming, someone *you* would like to meet for lunch.

Age

This may be the touchiest subject of all. Reading through 50+ Personals, you may notice that while men almost always state their age or age range, many women do not. Age is at the center of the dating anxieties felt by many 50+ women and however these anxieties are expressed, they boil down to the same basic concern: Am I still sexually attractive?

We've all seen the young "trophy" wives of middle-aged or elderly business tycoons. And we've all been to the movies. Robert Redford's leading lady in a recent film was thirty-eight to his sixty-three. Woody Allen's leading lady in a recent film was thirty-five to his sixty-five. The twenty-something Gwyneth Paltrow was the leading lady chosen for the fifty-something ac-tor Michael Douglas in one of his recent films.

Not that there's anything new about this. It's part of Hollywood tradition. Remember the pairing of the young Audrey Hepburn with the much, much older Fred Astaire, Humphrey Bogart, Rex Harrison, Gary Cooper, and Cary

Grant? Okay, Cary Grant was ageless, but the others? Remember Grace Kelly and Bing Crosby? Marilyn Monroe and Laurence Olivier? I could go on, but you get the point.

The implicit attitude is that young women are sexy, whereas older women are not. Listen to Tony Curtis, 74, on the subject: "I could never be married to a woman my own age. I'm forty-five years older than my wife and I haven't been this happy in a long time. Because of her, I feel like a thirty-year-old newlywed."

But most of us don't live in the world of tycoons and movie stars. In the real world, the good news for 50+ women is that the majority of men who place Personal ads are seeking someone their own age. Why should a man prefer a woman his own age? Because he wants a relationship with an equal. Because he doesn't want to start a second or third family. Because he wants a helpmate as well as a soul mate. Because he doesn't want to have to explain what the Beatles meant to a generation, or for that matter what the Big Bands meant to a generation. Because he wants a companion as well as a lover. Because he doesn't want to hold in his stomach for the rest of his life.

- John West: "I prefer women close to my own age because we share the same frame of reference."

- Stan Hewes: "I may look at the twenty-year-olds and thirty-year-olds, but I go out with women my own age. We have the same memories, we've been through the same kinds of things. It's comfortable. I don't have to pretend to be someone I'm not, or to be interested in things I don't give a damn about."

- Will Simon: "Dating younger women feels like incest."

- Paul Blythe: "I'm a better lover now than when I was thirty. Women my age are also better lovers now than when they were thirty."

The very good news for 50+ men is that the majority of 50+ women who place Personal ads care far more about inner qualities than looks, height, or age. Ask the classic question—What do women want?—and women answer without hesitation: "Integrity," "a man who knows how to share," "a man who makes me think," "a man who makes me laugh," "a man with an understanding heart," "a man with a loving spirit."

Don't let things like weight or height or age keep you from using the Personals. It may seem like romance is only for the young, thin, and beautiful, but that's not true. Be yourself, construct an honest set of priorities, and you will find what you're looking for.

Nancy Fedder advises women not to mention marriage in their ads "because men get scared." Instead she suggests such phrases as "committed relationship" or "serious relationship" which are specific but not threatening.

Women can also be put off by the "M" word. Sharon Freedman, Director of Development for a non-profit organization, won't respond to a Personal ad that mentions marriage. "It's inappropriate, too needy." Ann Sayre says, "It puts too much pressure on the situation. How can you relax if you feel you're being sized up as wife material? It's better to say 'long-term relationship.' That's clear enough. You don't have to hit anybody over the head."

It's easier than you may think. Look through the ads included in this book and then start to experiment with different ideas and phrases of your own. Your headline should reflect the thoughts in your ad and, above all, should reflect your personality. Write it *after* you've written your ad, not before. To help inspire you, here are some sample headlines:

- A Great Catch Who Wants to Get Caught

- Fun & Fantasy

- Smart Is Sexy

- Good Heart, Good Guy

- Great Laugh, Great Legs

- Fabulous at 52

- Holding Hands at Sunset

- Beauty & Brains

- Sassy, Silly, Smart, Sexy

- Do You Love Life?

- Love, Laughter, Hugs Available

- Be the Last Love of My Life

- Can You Make My Heart Smile?

- Welcome to My Life

"Welcome to My Life" needn't be your headline but it should be the attitude you bring to your search for someone new. Open your mind and heart and be ready for something good to happen.

If it doesn't happen right away, don't give up hope. Examine your ad and see what should be added or subtracted, what could be improved. Don't be afraid to ask for advice. If you're a man seeking a woman, ask a woman friend or relative what she thinks of your ad. If you're a woman seeking a man, ask a man. Whatever you do, keep trying.

CHAPTER 7

HOW TO DEAL WITH THE RESPONSES YOU RECEIVE

WHETHER RESPONSES FLOOD IN OR TRICKLE IN, you have to be prepared. Here are some practical suggestions:

STEPHANIE SIMMS: "I received about 150 responses to my online Personal. I didn't know I was going to get that many, but I'd worked out a system in advance because I was taking it seriously and I wanted to do it right. It's a four-part system.

1. I sent the same standard reply to everybody who contacted me the first time.

2. I sent a second standard reply to everybody who contacted me a second time.

3. After the second round of replies, the numbers started to get whittled down. The original 150 became 20, and I sent a personal reply to all 20.

4. The numbers finally got whittled down to 6, and then I was really able to communicate one-on-one.

"The whole procedure took about two months. It was worth it because I knew that the men who stayed with it were as serious as I was. In those two months they got a good idea of who I was and I got a good idea of who they were. We built a real connection. That's what I wanted. I wasn't in a hurry to talk on the phone or make a date to meet anybody. I knew if it was right it would still be right months later.

"Some men didn't understand that, but most did. One man was so anxious to prove his good intentions he sent me his Social Security number, his phone number, his driver's license number, and pages and pages about himself. Sometimes men surprise you.

"Right now I'm in contact with 2 of the original 150 men. One of them lives a distance away so we haven't met yet, but we will. I feel good about both of these men. The thing is I have high ideals and morals. These men understand that."

JERRY PHILLIPS: "I have a very simple strategy. One, I follow my own screening criteria (everybody has their own because everybody is interested in different things). Two, I always request a photo. If someone doesn't send a photo, I assume there's a reason and I don't respond."

NANCY FEDDER: "Toss the obvious mismatches, toss anything that makes you feel even slightly uncomfortable, but hold on to the others. Study them carefully before deciding yes, no, or maybe. Because you never know."

CHAPTER 8

PLUG IN
YOUR RADAR

WHEN YOU WERE A CHILD, YOUR MOTHER TOLD you never to talk to strangers. You've given the same warning to your own children and grandchildren. Now, at 50+, and thanks to the Personals, you will not only be talking to strangers, you will be making dates to meet them. So here's another warning: Be careful out there.

We all know that people aren't always what they seem. We know that the nastiest intentions can hide behind the nicest smiles. We know that good manners and good clothes can mask a multitude of sins. We know that the world can be a dangerous place. We know these things, but we forget. And when romance comes into the picture, well, who wants to spoil it by thinking dark thoughts?

Of course, most people are who and what they say they are. They have no secret agendas, no sinister plans. Like you, they simply want to connect, to find a companion, a soul mate, a relationship, a new life. Still, a stranger is a stranger and caution is advised. Proceed slowly. Use your instincts. Ask questions (ask, don't interrogate) and listen to the answers. Remember that the someone you've just met, whether by e-mail or snail mail or telephone, may be as wary as you are, so be patient.

Be sensible. A phrase sometimes used by American presidents to define elements of foreign policy can be useful in helping you define elements of your Personals policy: "Trust but verify."

Scientists have an explanation for why we feel an attraction to a specific person, to Joe Smith instead of Joe Jones, to Jane Smith instead of Jane Jones. It's encoded in our makeup, they say. It's in the neurotransmitter dopamine, in the hormones norepinephrine and vasopressin, and in the enzyme oxytocin. These transmitters and hormones and enzymes may also explain why otherwise intelligent people turn into idiots at the first sign of romance. No one is safe from this phenomenon. It doesn't matter how old we are or what we've accomplished in life, we're all vulnerable.

A nursing supervisor, she had been widowed for several years before meeting Robert through the Personals. "I felt isolated after my husband died. Our whole social life was as a couple. If we went out with friends or went to a barbecue, anything we did was like Noah's Ark, always two by two. Then all of a sudden it was just me. I wasn't half of a couple anymore; I was a widow, a single woman.

"If people invited me to a dinner party, they felt they needed to invite an extra man. If they couldn't find an extra man, they didn't invite me at all. That happened a lot. They didn't know what to do with me and I didn't know what to do with myself. That was part of the problem.

"The other part was that I wasn't used to much attention. My husband was a good man, but he wasn't what you'd call the touchy-feely type.

"I answered Robert's ad in our community newspaper. From the first moment we met he just *showered* me with attention. It was as if he hung on my every word. I look back on it now and I see how stupid I was, but at the time it didn't seem stupid. It seemed like a miracle. Here was this terrific man who was actually interested in what I thought about things, who actually seemed to care what I thought. He was always giving me little presents, just wanting to make me happy. Or at least that's what he said. He was always telling me he loved me.

"We were together a little over two months, and then one day he was gone. He left me a message about having to go out of town to see his daughter. I believed him. Even when I didn't hear from him, I believed him. After a couple of weeks it occurred to me that he wasn't coming back. I tried to find him. He'd moved out of his apartment, which turned out to be a sublet. No forwarding address, no new phone number, nothing. Then by accident I discovered my good jewelry was missing.

"That's when the light began to dawn. I went through my desk. Two of my credit cards were missing, along with some blank checks and my bank card. He knew I kept my pin numbers in my desk because I'd told him that's where I kept all my important papers. *That's* how stupid I was. In a way, I was his accomplice."

JOY'S STORY

The New York Times recently related the sad tale of a divorced teacher who lived with her two teenaged children in her mother's cramped Bronx home. She wanted to meet a gentle, decent man, preferably a man with the financial savvy to help her buy a home of her own. But when she responded to a Personal ad in *New York Magazine*, she became one of nine victims of a con man who ultimately swindled her out of a lot of money.

The man who placed the ad turned out to be "an athletically built charmer" who was especially eager to help Joy solve her financial problems. Her trust was strengthened by the Lexus he drove and by the fact that his brother was supposedly "a genius at investment." Alas, rather than finding the man of her dreams, she wound up putting all of her savings and her mother's savings into a string of business ventures that prosecutors have called fictitious.

In a period of three years, at least nine suburban women—mostly widowed or divorced professionals, one of them a Phi Beta Kappa—were persuaded to hand over considerable sums of money to the brothers. According to Michael Cherkasky, the president of Kroll Associates, the nation's largest investigative agency, Joy and the other women were victims of a pyramid scheme built on Personal ads and dating services. "These con men deliberately preyed on women who were desperate for companionship, who put reason behind them when they thought they'd found a mate. And the fact that the women were intelligent had nothing to do with it. They left their intelligence at the door of romance."

Joy concurs. "I ask myself time and time again how my mother and I could have been cheated so easily. When people are needy and desperate, they're gullible and grasp at straws. And if the straws don't make sense they fill in the pieces to make them make sense."

Advice from Joy: "Don't mix romance and money. If he offers to help you with your investments, run!"

The head of fundraising at a small college in the Northwest, he made his first foray into the Personals three years ago. "I made mistakes and I wound up in a very bad situation. It was a real 'Fatal Attraction,' except nobody got killed.

"My ad was straightforward. I was looking for an independent, sincere woman, college-educated. I said I preferred weight in proportion to height and that all respondents would be answered. I don't remember if I said anything about age, but anyway I heard from eleven women.

"This particular woman—the Fatal Attractionist or FA for short—was the third woman I met. She was younger than the others and younger than I. I won't say how much younger, but she was young enough to have a three-year-old daughter. She was pretty, pleasant, well-endowed in all the right places. She was on the quiet side, but not boring. You could describe her as quiet and low-key, very neat and nice. Not shy, but quiet. A single mother. But I liked two other women I met through my ad better. I enjoyed their company more.

"FA and I met for dinner and afterwards I walked her to her car, took her hand, and thanked her for the evening. I knew and she knew that I wasn't going to call her again. There wasn't anything wrong with her. I was just more interested in the other women. They were a better match for me.

"The very next night FA called me at home from a pay phone nearby and asked me to meet her. I told her I was busy and thanked her for calling. I still wasn't interested and she knew it. The next night she called again. She was at the same pay phone and asked would I meet her? She sounded so eager, as if she could hardly wait to see me. Well, the other women weren't calling me, and here FA had called two nights in a row."

Mistake No. 1: "I was flattered by the attention from a younger woman and I let that color my thinking. I agreed to meet her.

"I drove over to where she was. It was a nice night. She got in the car and we went for a drive. After a while she asked to see where I lived. When we got there, she asked to see my apartment. Usually that would be a no-brainer; sure, come on in. But this time my first instinct was to say no. I still don't know why. I was flattered and she was attractive. But there was something that bothered me. Maybe it was because she was pushing too hard. I don't know. Whatever it was, my instinct said to say no."

Mistake No. 2: "I ignored my instinct and asked her in. I got her a soft drink and we sat on the couch and talked. There was some snuggling, some kissing, but nothing else. That's the truth. An hour later I drove her back to her car.

"I'd decided not to call her. It wasn't anything specific. It was just a feeling—something seemed not right. I didn't call her but she started calling me. Once a week, then a couple of times a week, then almost every night. I didn't know what to think. She didn't seem the kind of woman to be so aggressive. Yet she kept calling. And I got into the habit of talking to her. She seemed to value my opinion on every subject. I admit it was good for my ego.

"Then, the next month, she moved from the city to my suburb. I didn't think anything of it at the time because it was a nicer neighborhood, much better for her daughter. I figured it was a natural evolution."

Mistake No. 3: "I wasn't thinking. I didn't put two and two together.

"After talking to her so much on the phone, I finally asked her out. We went out twice. Dinner, a movie; nothing special. I liked her well enough. I felt flattered by all the attention she was paying to me. Well, one thing led to another and we hit the sack after the third date. But I still had the uncomfortable feeling that something wasn't right. I couldn't shake it.

"I began to back away from FA. I didn't talk to her so much on the phone—sometimes I just didn't answer the phone, other times I answered and told her I was on my way out. I didn't see her for a while. Instead I got back in touch with the first woman I'd met through my ad. We had a couple of dates. I really enjoyed this woman's company and it was mutual. A few weeks passed.

"The next time I saw FA, I was honest. I said I didn't think it was working out for us, I didn't think there was a future. I talked about the age difference, things like that. She said she understood, and that we should stay friends. It was very amicable. I was relieved. I figured that was the end of it.

"But then strange things started happening. About a month after I broke it off with FA, I started getting hang-ups when I answered the phone. My garbage was stolen. The breakers in my fuse box were tripped. My mail was torn up and scattered on the driveway. A rock was thrown through my window. It was a lot of different things one right after the other. Small things in the beginning. I thought it was probably kids and their pranks. After the incident with the rock, I knew it was more serious than that. FA crossed my mind when all this was going on, but I never really believed she was behind it."

Mistake No. 4: "I still wasn't thinking. I didn't see the obvious.

"I spent Christmas in another city. When I got back home after my trip I went straight to bed. The bell rang minutes later. I went downstairs and looked through the peephole. FA said she knew I was there and please open the door. She said she was cold standing outside, that she wanted to give me a Christmas present and then she would leave. I opened the door. When she came in she was wearing a mid-length winter coat. I asked her where the present was. She held the coat open and said 'Merry Christmas.' Yep, she was naked. You can guess what happened next."

Mistake No. 5: "I was thinking with the wrong part of my body.

"After that, the real trouble began. One morning I left my apartment and found FA standing outside. She was dirty and disheveled, wearing rumpled old clothes. As soon as she saw me she started screaming. 'Why haven't you called me?' and 'I've been going crazy,' and then the kicker, 'I'm pregnant.' I tried to talk to her, to calm her down, but she just kept screaming. It nearly stopped my heart, I was so stunned. I'd never seen her that way before and suddenly I realized she was the one who'd been doing all those strange things.

"I kept trying to talk to her but it was no use, so I jumped in my car and drove away. She jumped in her car and followed me. After that day she seemed to follow me everywhere I went.

"I asked a friend to run a record check on FA for criminal and work history—I had to know who I was dealing with. Well, she had a rap sheet a mile long: embezzlement, theft, fraud, forgery, burglary, etc. At the time, she was apparently living on part-time jobs and the child support her child's father paid.

"I finally located the father. I'll call him 'Ed.' I told Ed my story and he told me his. FA stalked him and every member of his family. His mother had to move to another state because of the harassment. His house mysteriously burned to the ground. It was arson but they never caught the perpetrator. Ed's advice to me was 'Get the hell away from her. Move if you have to, but get away.' I was stunned all over again. I couldn't believe I'd gotten myself into such a mess.

"Within a week of my conversation with Ed, FA moved again. Her new apartment was three blocks away from me. One day she ambushed me on the sidewalk and yelled that she wasn't pregnant anymore, that she'd had an abortion and it was all my fault.

"She followed me everywhere—to work, to the grocery store, the post office. Whenever I looked around, she was there. I'd changed my telephone number but somehow she got the new one and she started calling every night, all night long, playing music on the phone—love songs over and over. Sometimes her voice was seductive, sultry. Most of the time she was screaming threats at me: she was going to go to the dean of my college and make a scene; she was going to smash my car windows and slash my tires; she was going to throw Drano in my face; she was going to kill me. I made three or four police reports about her threats, but the cops just thought it was stupid. 'A man like you can't control some *woman*? What's the matter with you?'

"The calls continued. The tirades continued. One night the doorbell rang; it was FA and I wouldn't let her in. She went to a pay phone and called me. I let the machine pick up. FA's message was that if I didn't let her in, she would break all the windows in my apartment. Ten minutes later baseball-sized rocks were coming through my windows. I called the police. She was gone when they arrived. Nothing they could do, they said.

"A week later she did go to the dean of my college and started screaming that he should ask me how many other women I was screwing. Only she didn't say 'screwing.' At the same time she started sending me packages of women's perfumed undergarments with sequined stars and hearts tossed in. In other circumstances it would have been a male fantasy come true. In these circumstances it was frightening.

"My car was broken into—cell phone, radar detector,

everything smashed to pieces. Was it FA? I thought so, but the cops said there was no proof.

"I had new locks installed on my car, my apartment doors, my fuse boxes, every place I could think of. I changed my phone number again and again FA got the new number. The calls started again. Love songs all night, over and over. If I took the phone off the hook, she threw rocks at the windows or threw paint on the driveway.

"One night I was standing in line at the supermarket and I heard a whisper behind me 'I've got six bullets with your name on them. Watch your back'. She turned and walked away.

"Another night I got home to find pry marks on my door and the foyer light smashed. Guess who?

"By then it was spring. One morning I got into my car just as FA pulled up behind me and blocked me in. I got out of my car. FA walked right up to me and hit me in the mouth. She started screaming 'Who's Janice?' (Janice was a woman I'd dated a couple of times and liked.) I shoved FA back into an adjacent car that had an alarm. Needless to say, that woke the whole apartment complex. I went back into my apartment and stayed there till I knew she was gone. How did FA know about Janice? She'd gone through my garbage and found some notes I'd written to myself.

"The stalking really got intense about that time. She was always there. I had to leave restaurants, ball games, stores, just to get away from her. I had to drive like a CIA agent to keep her from ramming my car. Somehow she found out where Janice lived. She showed up there one night, circling the block and honking the horn until we called the police. That night the cops showed up in time and asked FA what her business was. She didn't have an answer, so the police informed her that she was stalking and would have to leave immediately. They told her that if she returned, she would be arrested. Janice was very upset, understandably, and didn't want to see me anymore. That was the end of that relationship.

"The worst night with FA happened in early summer. She was following my car and I just wanted to lose her. When the light changed, I sped away and turned into a side street. I drove another block and turned the car around, facing the street exit, waiting for FA to pass. It was dark. My lights were out, and I could see her cruising up the street, looking for my car. She passed right next to me before she realized it. My motor was already running. I put it in gear and sped off. She tried to back up into me to keep me from getting away, but she couldn't turn quickly enough. I was sure I'd lost her. I kept driving along, then about eight blocks later I saw her car coming at me. *Coming straight at me*. I swerved. We missed a head-on collision by inches. I just stopped the car and dropped my head on the steering wheel. The next thing I knew, FA was standing beside my car, saying she had a gun and was going to kill me. I put the car in gear again and took off. I really was at the end of my rope. When I got home, I locked all the doors, turned out the lights, and just sat there, wondering what I was going to do.

"A couple of days later, I was amazed to see FA's picture on the front page of our local newspaper. It seemed that while she was out stalking and tailing me, she'd left her young daughter at home and the child had wandered out of the house. She'd been found in the middle of the street by a neighbor and the police had been called. When FA arrived home, she'd been arrested.

"I knew this was my chance—maybe my only chance—to get rid of the problem once and for all. Child abandonment was a serious charge she wouldn't be able to wriggle out of. That night I called the detective working the case and gave him all the background information. I told him I would be glad to repeat it at FA's hearing.

"On the day of the hearing, I confronted FA and her court-appointed lawyer. In addition, it turned out that I knew the presiding judge. Finally, some luck had come my way! The judge ruled that that she had to undergo counseling, and that she sever all ties to me. She was told that she had to satisfy all the conditions of her probation if she hoped to regain custody of her daughter. I was free!

"Well, not quite. That same afternoon FA followed me all the way to my door, saying 'we had to talk.' But I'd had enough, and this time I knew the law was on my side. It was all in the court records. The whole story. So I got my door open, stopped, turned, looked around for witnesses (there were none), and shoved her a good twelve to fifteen feet into the yard and onto her back. This time I was in charge of the situation. I told her I had a gun now (I lied) and if she came near me again I'd kill her. I told her that now that the court knew my story, I could kill her and get away with it. From the shocked look on FA's face, I knew she believed me. Finally, I knew I was really free. Bottom line, she never bothered me again.

"A postscript: Months later, a neighbor told me he saw FA in a restaurant, sitting with a man at the bar. We both laughed. FA was someone else's problem now!"

Advice from Larry: "Don't let your ego get in the way of common sense. If something feels wrong to you, something *is* wrong. Don't dig a hole for yourself."

She is a divorced sales rep in Florida and began e-mail correspondence with a man named Jess after reading his profile on an online Personals site. "He seemed interesting, a television executive with funny stories to tell. We wrote back and forth. He sent me his phone numbers for home and work, but it was a couple of months before I called him. I was feeling very low—my son was having problems at school—and I suddenly felt like talking to Jess. I called his home number and left a message on his machine.

"He called me back the next day and we started talking. He was wonderful. Understanding, sensitive, intelligent, bright, funny. Too good to be true! We continued talking for about three weeks and then he said he was coming to Florida to visit his mother and to attend to some business. He also said he had very strong feelings for me (as I had for him) just from the phone calls. He wanted to meet me and take me out. We made a date for the night after Valentine's Day.

"He was going to pick me up at the office in a limousine and the whole office was in an uproar, excited for me, because it seemed like everything was perfect. He sent flowers and his picture before the date. The card that came with the flowers said 'Can't wait to meet you.' On the appointed day he showed up in a huge limousine with a gift bag of Valentine's presents. We had a night to remember—dinner at Planet Hollywood, a drive through South Beach, drinks at a café. He was so charming. He even brought a gift for my son and said he wanted to get to know him too.

"He gave me his résumé so I could see what he'd accomplished. I was really impressed but scared to death at the same time because I had been hurt so often before. After Jess went back to California, we talked every day on the phone for about three weeks. He always called when he said he would and it was getting better with each call. He came back to Florida specifically to see me about a month later. We went out for dinner to the best steak house in town and spent the entire next day together before he went home again. Before he left, I asked him if he would like to take me to my daughter's wedding, which was two months away. He said he would love to do that. I was thrilled.

"For the next two months he continued to call every day from California. He asked what kind of car I wanted to go to the wedding in, a Rolls, limo, or town car. He asked for the correct spelling of my daughter's name so he could send a gift check. He told me he would come to Florida on the Thursday before the wedding, so we could have some time together before the Saturday ceremony. I was so excited. It was going to be a wonderful day for my daughter and a wonderful day for me. Well, maybe you can guess the rest.

"Jess didn't show up on Thursday or Friday. When I tried to call him, I found out that all his numbers had been disconnected. I couldn't find him; he'd disappeared without a trace. I wound up driving myself to the wedding in an old Toyota and had to stop to pick up two people to boot!

"It was another two months before Jess surfaced again, and then only because I'd left a couple of messages at his mother's house. My son left a message too, saying how upset I was about everything. After those messages Jess called and screamed at me—how dare I call his mother, etc., etc. It was awful. I couldn't match that angry, shouting man to the sensitive man I'd known. Or *thought* I'd known.

"We talked on the phone several times after that. He kept making promises that never came true. I checked out the references on his résumé—none of them had ever heard of him. I kept hoping against hope that there was some reasonable explanation for everything, hoping there was still a chance for us.

"The straw that broke the camel's back was when he returned to Florida. We'd made a date to meet; I was supposed to call him on his cell phone after I finished at work. When I called the number, I got a completely different person, not Jess, and I just lost it. I was so mad and upset. Jess called me at home that night, screaming at me again—how dare I call him—but I screamed right back. I told him I knew his references were phony, I knew he was phony. I just wanted to know why he'd done these things? *Why?*

"I never got an explanation. He hung up and I never heard from him again. The only explanation I can think of is that he's nuts. But whatever it is, it doesn't matter anymore. I will not allow myself to ever get hurt again. I've sworn off men!"

Advice from Nan: "Don't believe everything you're told. Check things out for yourself."

❧ Is He Married? ❧

E-mail offers a seductive blend of anonymity and intimacy. The anonymity factor lessens and even eliminates inhibitions. The intimacy factor fosters an easy exchange of confidences, allowing a "relationship" to develop very quickly. After a few days of e-mail correspondence you may think you know him. You don't.

E-mail has been likened to "confiding in someone behind a dark screen." This is both romantic and risky. There's the undeniable lure of the Mysterious Stranger, but there's also the potential to deceive. A "dark screen" can be a hiding place for con men, for imposters. For married men. Are you thinking that 50+ women are exempt from the married man problem? Think again.

MICHELLE'S STORY

A widow who works as a stock broker in an Eastern city, she began an e-mail correspondence with a 50+ man who visited her city once a month on business. They corresponded for several weeks—sometimes for hours at a time—then arranged to meet during his next visit.

"We bypassed the telephone completely. Thinking back, I can't remember why. He must have come up with good reasons and obviously I accepted them. We went directly from e-mail to our first date. That was a terrible mistake. If I'd insisted on talking to him on the phone, I'm sure it would have ended right then and there. He wouldn't have been able to give me his home phone number and I would have put two and two together. Everything is always so clear in hindsight, isn't it?

"The truth is I was already emotionally involved by the time we met. Do men *ever* get emotionally involved? I wonder about that...I felt so close to this man. I'd really opened up to him. He knew everything about me. At the time I thought I knew everything about him. I believed, *really, really believed*, I'd found someone I could spend the rest of my life with. This is where I should type in LOL! (Laugh Out Loud).

"We met and everything was perfect. He was all I'd imagined he'd be (don't underestimate the power of imagination). We had the most wonderful time. I don't think there was any doubt in either of our minds that we would make love that night. And we did. That was perfect, too. Everything I'd fantasized and more. It wasn't until after we'd made love that he told me he was married.

"I was crushed. I mean *crushed*. Any devastating thing you can think of, that's what it was like. I realized I didn't know this man at all. I realized what a jerk I'd been. The worst part, I could see all my dreams just crumbling and falling to pieces. It was awful for me.

"It turned out that this man had four different e-mail addresses and was corresponding with four different women. His wife didn't have a clue."

She is an Easterner who began an e-mail correspondence with a 50+ Midwestern man who often traveled to her city on business. She says, "I sit here staring at the skyline and I think of worlds out there that we never know existed until we crash into them.

"A year ago I began an innocent online conversation with a complete stranger. The chatting is something we are all familiar with in cyberspace, but this was different right from the start. The chat room that 'Mark' was in wasn't of much interest to me, but I was feeling sassy, so I entered and asked a few silly questions. I ended up meeting the most sincere, thoughtful, and intelligent man I've ever known. A man with great compassion and insight. We found an incredible degree of intimacy together. We sent videos and pictures to each other. He called me every day and we talked online every night. He sent me tapes of his favorite music. He sent me books and poetry. We lived far away from each other and yet we felt closer to each other than we had ever felt to anyone else in our lives. We fell in love. Yes. We fell in love.

"It was a little while before I found out he was married. I can't say it was a complete surprise—he had a post office box for his mail, and he never gave me his home telephone number. I can say that it didn't change my feelings for him. I was in love. I'm still in love.

"A month after we met online we started planning to meet in person. It was so exciting. I still remember the butterflies in my stomach when we talked the morning of his flight...'Gonna be there soon, and I can't wait to hold you in my arms…' And the butterflies when I was driving to the airport! He was so beautiful standing there. He saw me first and we just smiled. I finally got the courage to touch him and prove to myself he was real.

"Walking together hand in hand, strolling through a park, stopping and folding into each other in a remarkably perfect fit. Falling in love, being in love is so wonderful—unless one of you still has children at home, adolescents who believe in who you are and what you stand for.

"I don't know how our story will turn out. I don't know how many years we have left to us. But we have a dream and I believe in it. We dream that one day, when his children are grown and gone, we will be together in our own house in the country. We dream that we will live out the rest of our lives together. I believe that somehow we will make our dream come true."

E-mail isn't the only venue for married men. They can be found in the print Personals too, sometimes identifying themselves as married men, sometimes not.

Paul's Story

A 52-year-old businessman, he has run three Personal ads in *Washingtonian Magazine* during the past five years. "Each of my ads said I was a married man seeking an honest, safe, discreet long-term relationship. I've never lied about being married. I'm always upfront about my situation.

"The fact is I got married for the wrong reasons and I've made a lot of mistakes in 25 years. I haven't been happy, but I have teenage children at home and I don't want to break up my family. I don't want to hurt anybody, but I need something for myself as well. Something more out of life.

"I've had two relationships since I ran my first Personal ad. I travel a good deal for business and I often work late, so there are many opportunities to meet. Dinner, a show, overnight at a good hotel, that's my idea of a nice evening. I can get away on weekends, so on a nice day, with the right woman, I like to walk through the woods holding hands, then later have dinner by the fire.

"I've learned how to please a woman in bed, but for me this isn't just about what happens between the sheets. That's easy. What I'm looking for isn't easy.

"I've never really been in love. I don't want to hurt anybody, but the truth is if I were ever to fall in love—to know love—there's nothing I wouldn't do to keep it."

JOHN'S STORY

He's 56 and lives on the East Coast. He's not looking for a serious relationship and he hasn't always identified himself as a married man. "I don't intend to leave my family. I don't want complications in my life. But when you've been married a long time, you need diversion. I've met six or seven women through the Personals and had affairs with three of them. One of them knew from the start that I was married. One of them figured it out for herself. The third one didn't know until I told her, and that was after we'd had a number of dates. I told her because she was starting to get serious. I'd let it go on too long and that was a mistake. I try not to make mistakes like that.

"I may not seem it, but I'm a cautious man. I travel a lot in my business, always to the same two cities. I only go out with women in those cities, never in my home city. I have a separate, private phone line that I say is my home phone, and I also have call forwarding to my private office line. I rent space at one of the mailbox places, in case I have to give an address. I don't feel as if I'm always looking over my shoulder, but I do try to be discreet.

"The main thing is I don't intend to leave my family."

There are married men like Paul and married men like John, but in their own ways they're all looking for "something more out of life." Make sure it's not you.

How can you avoid entangling yourself in an unpleasant situation? Imagine a grid with boundary lines well-defined by red flags. Each flag represents a warning. For example, let's say you've met someone through the Personals. Perhaps you're still at the e-mail/letter/phone call stage, or perhaps you've already had your first face-to-face meeting. Whatever stage you're at, you're feeling good about it because you see potential there. And yet somewhere in the back of your mind something is worrying you. Some small, nagging doubt you can't quite define but can't quite get rid of, either.

Let's say, for example, that the person you've met is in far too much of a hurry to move things along. You feel flattered but you also feel uncomfortable. You feel pressured, and you start wondering if the person you've met is too needy or too desperate or too unsure or too controlling? That's a *red flag*.

Or let's say the person you've met asks inappropriate questions about your finances or makes inappropriate sexual remarks. It happens more than once and you start wondering if it's just social clumsiness due to nerves, or if something else is going on? That's a *red flag*.

Or let's say the person you've met is too sketchy, too evasive about the basic facts of his or her life. You start wondering what the mystery is? Is there some deep, dark secret? That's a *red flag*.

Or let's say the person you've met seems moody. A sudden flash of anger, a sudden manic outburst, a sudden down-in-the-dumps funk. You start wondering what to make of it—emotional instability, drugs, what? That's a *red flag*.

Or let's say the person you've met shows early signs of being possessive. You start wondering if you'll be expected to detail your comings and goings, to account for your time. That's a *red flag*.

Anything that worries you is a *red flag*. Treat it accordingly, use it as a warning to keep your eyes and ears open. If you accumulate more than one *red flag*, stop and reassess the situation. Express your doubts and ask a few direct questions. If you don't get the right answers or if you get no answers at all, break it off.

At 50+ you have better things to do with your time than waste it on phonies and schemers, so take a breath and move on. There may not be plenty of other fish in the sea but there *are* other fish. A good fisherperson needs only two things—patience and the right bait.

CHAPTER 9

HOW DO YOU DEAL WITH THE UNEXPECTED?

IT'S TRUE WHAT THEY SAY ABOUT THE BEST-LAID plans going astray. You can make a dozen lists, tie up a hundred loose ends, and follow your strategy point by point, but things still may not turn out precisely the way you envisioned them. Don't let that throw you. Do as much as you can to produce the results you want and then let the universe take over.

One of the great things about the Personals is that they give you control. How often in life can you say that something is entirely up to you? Not often, but don't let that go to your head. In the Personals, as in life, there are going to be surprises along the way.

You start as strangers, exchanging letters or e-mail. You start imagining what your stranger will be like when you meet. You can anticipate, you can fantasize, you can hope, but you can't know for sure. The person who comes to meet you may not match the photo you've seen or the description you've been given. How important is this? It depends.

Lee Willets' Story

A Texan, Lee replied to the Personal ad of a woman who described herself as a "Rita Hayworth look-alike." "I kept building up a picture in my mind, so there was a lot of anticipation by the time we met. Then when we did meet, I just felt a lot of disappointment. She was just a woman with a wide mouth and a lot of dyed red hair. I would have got over the disappointment—I mean, if you're dumb-ass enough to really be expecting Rita Hayworth, you deserve whatever happens to you. But what I didn't like was that this woman saw herself as Rita. I kept wondering, doesn't she have a mirror? Or was she one of those women who was always trying to be something she's not? I've known women like that and they're not for me."

DEBRA STERN'S STORY

She is a nutritionist who lives in New Jersey. Like Lee, the person she met wasn't the person she had imagined; unlike Lee, her experience ended happily. "Looks aren't primary to me, but I've always had a certain type I was drawn to. I expected Andy to be that type, but when we met I saw he was exactly the opposite. He had a beard and longer hair than I liked. He was very quiet and didn't smile much. He wasn't what I was expecting at all. Yet there was something about him. There must have been, because instead of doing my usual thing—which was having a cup of coffee and then leaving as fast as I could—I stayed to talk to him. We talked for a long time. We didn't have everything in common, but we never ran out of conversation. We still haven't and we've been together three years. I'm so thankful I stayed. Look what I would have missed!"

∞ ARE YOU PICKY, PICKY, PICKY? ∞

It's a fact of life—no matter what you do, there's just no pleasing some people. John Tierney, writing in *The New York Times Magazine*, advances the theory, only half in jest, that some singles are afflicted with "what I call the Flaw-O-Matic. You can think of the Flaw-O-Matic as an inner voice, a little whirring device that instantly spots a fatal flaw in any potential mate. This phenomenon, while most prevalent in New York, is found in other places too."

Sad to say, the Flaw-O-Matic can be found in a lot of 50+ singles. Sometimes it's a defense mechanism. 50+ers who have been widowed after happy marriages feel guilty about finding love again. Julie Reyes, a 61-year-old insurance broker, had been a widow for more than a year when she first tried the Personals. "I knew it was time to start living my life again and I wasn't meeting anybody any other way, so I started looking at Personal ads. I actually met a few nice men, but the problem was that I felt disloyal to my late husband. In a crazy way I felt like I was cheating on him. And I was a terrible date! I made all the classic mistakes. Talked too much. Talked too much about my marriage. Once I even burst into tears. I was embarrassed, but I learned from that experience. I learned the world doesn't come to an end if you make a big fool of yourself.

"Another thing I learned is that everything is a process. You have to go through the steps. After I stopped boring all my dates to death with stories about my marriage, I moved on to the next step. Which was finding fault with all my dates. I could always find something wrong, even if it was just the color of his tie. I learned that you can talk yourself out of anything or anyone. Don't do that. Because if you do, you'll talk yourself out of happiness."

The same advice applies to people who have had bad marriages or relationships. In that situation it's not a question of disloyalty, it's a question of risk. You may want to meet someone new and start over but do you dare risk your heart again? Once burned, twice wary. And if you've been burned more than once, the wariness factor can be huge. Instead of examining your feelings, it's easier to plug in the old Flaw-O-Matic. If you're a woman, you can decide you don't like his taste in clothes or aftershave. If you're a man, you can decide you don't like the way she smiles or wears her hair or walks into a room. Any little thing will do.

Whether you're blessed with happy memories or cursed with memories from hell, don't deliberately put obstacles in the way of a new relationship. If you sense this is what you're doing, call a time out and think about it. The Personals can set you on the right road but you have to be ready, willing, and able to take the next steps on your own. Don't squander your opportunities. Squander not, want not.

Of course some people are picky by nature. To be fair, it should be said that by the time we reach 50+, we're all picky about something or other. That's fine, but keep it in perspective. Tempting as it might be to think you can design a soul mate to specification, it doesn't work that way. A soul mate is part chemistry, part compatibility, part understanding, part attitude, part intangibility, part serendipity. It can happen in an instant or it can happen over time, but it won't happen if you stick to a laundry list of criteria. Repeat after me—there's no such thing as a perfect person.

Here's the scenario. You've been having a great time exchanging e-mails or letters with someone who is as yet unknown to you. You've had a few great phone conversations with this same someone, so you make a date to meet. You can hardly wait, *because this could be the one*. And then you meet. And then you know. This is the one, all right. This is the date from hell. Can it happen to you? Yes, it can happen to anyone.

JOANNA FRANK'S STORY

"I hadn't had many dates since my divorce. I ran a Personal ad and Tom was one of the men who wrote to me. I liked his letter very much. He had interesting things to say, and he'd obviously given the letter a lot of thought. I liked that, too. Then we spoke on the phone maybe half a dozen times. Very good conversations. I felt at ease with him. I thought we were in sync. I was absolutely looking forward to meeting him.

"Well, we met and it was terrible. He was nice enough at first, but he kept patting his jacket pocket over and over again and when I looked more closely I saw that there were packets of condoms sticking out of his pocket. Right there in plain sight. I couldn't believe it. I finally asked him what he was doing and he made a really tasteless remark. It wasn't funny or clever, it was just tasteless. This wasn't the man I'd liked so much on the phone. Or I guess this was the real him and the man on the phone was an invention. I'll make a long story short—he made another remark, an obscene remark, and he said it loud enough for the people around us at other tables to hear. I was mortified. I left as quickly as I could and didn't look back.

"It wasn't the remarks in themselves that upset me—I'm a big girl, I've heard remarks like that before. It was that I'd been so wrong about him. What kind of man has condoms hanging out of his pocket when he goes to meet a woman for the first time? A jerk, obviously. It gave me a creepy feeling."

"I had high hopes when I went to meet Fred. In our phone conversations he'd seemed like a very understanding person. My husband had left me, walked out on our marriage for the usual reason, a younger woman. It was hard for me to accept. It was hell, if you want to know the truth.

"Fred seemed to understand that. This will sound silly, but he seemed protective of me. That wasn't all, though. He was funny, he had a nice sense of humor. I hadn't laughed in a long time, so I did have high hopes.

"The first thing I noticed when we met was that he was much older than he had claimed. I'm in my late fifties, Fred was probably in his seventies. But the worst thing was that he'd had so much plastic surgery he hardly looked human. My heart sank down to my knees. There was a mirrored panel behind me and he kept looking at his reflection. He'd be talking to me and then his eyes would move to the mirror. That's how the whole conversation went. I sat there longer than I should have, because I wanted to give him the benefit of the doubt. But he never stopped looking at himself in the mirror.

"We walked for a few blocks after we left the restaurant. There were no mirrors, so he kept checking out his reflection in store windows instead. That was enough for me. He wanted to take me home, but I said no thanks. As nicely as I could, I told him it wasn't going to work out for us. When he walked away, I saw him stop in front of a plate glass window and kind of lean into it, smoothing his hair while he studied his reflection. I didn't know whether to laugh or cry."

Another down-to-earth Texan, he responded to a Personal ad online. "Elaine's photo looked great and when we finally talked on the phone we had great conversations, so I was feeling good about meeting her in person. For about the first ten minutes it was fine, better than fine. I was already congratulating myself for making a good choice.

"Then she started. She liked my watch—what did it cost? She liked my suit—where did I buy it and was it expensive? What kind of car did I drive—did I own it or lease it? Was my house free and clear? I asked her did she want a bank statement and three financial references—just kidding her—but for a while there I thought she was going to take me up on it.

"She kept talking about money all through dinner. What did this cost, what did that cost? Was I in the stock market? What kind of pension funds did I have? She said that at our age money was the first priority. Maybe so, but I wasn't there to cut a business deal. We finished dinner, I walked her to her car and that was it. She called me once or twice, but I never called her back. I'd hate to think of spending my life with a woman who has dollar signs for eyes."

A college administrator in New York, her marriage of 26 years ended in divorce. "I had seven or eight dates through the Personals, but only one really appealed to me. Al was articulate and witty. I liked him and we got along very well.

"Maybe I should have realized there was a problem. One day we were walking in a park and heard a helicopter buzzing around in the sky. He stopped, froze, and said 'I hate that sound.' He'd been in Vietnam and associated the sound with his experiences there. I didn't think too much about it at the time; everybody who was in that war has bad memories. How could they not?

"For our third date I invited Al to my house for dinner. I didn't plan anything extra fancy, but I wanted to make it nice for both of us—our first dinner at home and all that. So I was a little surprised by what he was wearing when he arrived. I don't know how to describe it except that he was all in combat gear with an army fatigue jacket. I thought it was odd, but I didn't say anything. We sat down, dinner was cooking, we were having a lovely time. I felt close to him. Close enough so that I wanted him to know more about me. I told him about a health problem I had, about a difficult family situation—things I thought he should know if we were going to go any further. I had put fresh sheets on the bed just in case we did.

"Al wasn't bothered by what I told him. We talked about it for a while. Then he said, 'Well, there's something you should know about me, too,' at which point he opened his jacket and I saw he was carrying a gun. I saw the gun, I saw the strange look on his face. All I could think was that my daughters were going to find me shot to death on the couch.

"He held his jacket open, keeping the gun in sight, waiting to hear my reaction. I couldn't think of anything to say. Finally, I said, 'I hope you like broccoli.' He didn't think that was very funny. He said I shouldn't make a joke of this. And again there was that strange look on his face. I apologized and after a little while he seemed to be okay. He didn't hurt me. We went ahead and had dinner, talking to each other as if those moments hadn't happened.

"I guess I assumed the gun was part of a post-traumatic stress syndrome, his way of feeling safe, but it was over for us. Al didn't call me again after that night and I was relieved. If I made a list of really bad dates, this one would go right up at the top!"

There's no lesson here, because almost everybody has had a date that would qualify as Top 10 All-Time-Bad. Get through it, laugh about it later, move on.

Never take a detour or a shortcut when it comes to personal safety. It's axiomatic that women have to be more careful than men, but no one should take chances. AOL's Romance Channel offers seven tried and true rules for personal safety in the Personals:

1. Even though you may feel you've come to know someone through online interaction, *do* remember that the people you meet online are in fact strangers.

2. *Don't* give out your telephone number or address while on-line. Guard your personal information.

3. *Don't* believe everything you read. It's very easy for someone to misguide you via online correspondence. Remember that the person on the other end may not be who he says he is.

4. *Don't* respond to any correspondence that's lewd or crude or in any way makes you feel uncomfortable. Many Internet service providers offer you the option of multiple screen names—or of changing your screen name—so you can switch if one of them keeps drawing unwanted e-mails. Use a different screen name if you are feeling uncomfortable. Ignore obscene e-mails and Instant Messages.

5. *Do* report any obscene e-mails you receive directly to your Internet provider.

6. If you choose to meet someone you've "met" online, *do* meet in a public place and, if possible, in a group setting.

7. Enjoy yourself, but do use good judgment and be sensible.

Apply the same rules to the print Personals, especially the ones about guarding personal information and meeting in public places. Women should not be quick to give out their addresses, last names, or home phone numbers. "I don't give out my phone number," says one New Jersey woman. "I get theirs. I disable their caller ID with Star 67, so if they do a Star 69, my number won't show up." Another East Coast woman insists on arranging a conference call among herself, her correspondent, and one of his female co-workers or neighbors, "just to verify the back story."

While these defensive measures may seem extreme, remember that it's always best to err on the side of caution. Do what makes you feel comfortable and if your correspondent balks, pass.

Peter Brent thinks there should be a happy medium between nonchalance and CIA-like secrecy. "Some women are too quick to send their phone numbers and last names. Obviously that's not a good idea. Other women are too slow to share that information and that's not a good idea, either. There should be a middle ground, something in between the two extremes. It's not comfortable to be on a third date with a woman and still not know her last name. I like to feel a certain level of trust with—and from—any woman I'm seeing."

Stan Hewes says, "I'm annoyed by the assumption that all men are rapists or ax murderers in waiting, but yes, women do have to be careful. They should set the rules and stick to them."

Jerry Phillips agrees (more or less). He offers women this half-kidding, half-serious word of advice: "Beware!"

Beware, but remember—common sense, yes; paranoia, no.

CHAPTER 10

THE BIG MOMENT

You're about to meet face to face for the first time. You're meeting in a public place, a place that's convenient for both of you to get to, and a place where you feel comfortable. You're meeting for coffee or a drink or lunch or brunch; you know that if the chemistry between you is bad, you can leave after half an hour or so without feeling awkward about it. You also know that if the chemistry is promising, you can extend your date indefinitely.

You and the someone you're meeting are strangers and yet you know basic things about each other: past or present jobs or careers, how many children or grandchildren are in your families, your hobbies and interests, your usual travel destinations. You know that you can fall back on any of these subjects if the conversation flags, but you have more interesting subjects in mind.

You're excited, because this could be the start of the new life you want. You're nervous, too. Palms feeling a little damp? Throat feeling a little dry? You're nervous because you don't really know what to expect. You wonder if it was a mistake to make this date. For a moment you think about turning around and walking right out the door. But you don't walk out. Instead you stand there, debating with yourself. Is it silly to start dating again at your age? Are you setting yourself up for disappointment? Are you making a fool of yourself?

You know how hard dating is ("War games" is how Jerry Phillips describes it and he's not far from wrong). You know all about the uncertainties and false starts. You know about the misunderstandings and missed connections. You know there's a chance you'll be hurt. These are the minuses. You think about the pluses. A chance to fall in love again. A chance to begin again. A chance to share your life with someone you love.

You ask yourself if the pluses outweigh the minuses. And in the end you know there is only one answer: Yes, yes, a thousand times, yes!

You walk to the table where your date is waiting and introduce yourself. "So nice to meet you," you say, and you smile.

∞ Do You Think I'm Sexy? ∞

It has already been noted that anxieties about age mask a more fundamental concern: Am I still sexually attractive? We live in a society that prizes youth and that until recently has treated sexuality as the province of twenty-somethings and thirty-somethings; in special cases, forty-somethings. Apart from well-worn caricatures (the lecherous male, the man-hungry female) in television sitcoms, 50+ sexuality has been virtually invisible in the media. No more.

Society still prizes youth, but there is a new willingness to acknowledge the fact that sexy is sexy at any age. Want proof? Just look at *Modern Maturity Magazine*'s 1999 list of "Top 50 Sexiest Celebs Over 50."

Steam Heat Sexy:

James Brolin • Richard Gere • Susan Sarandon

Tropical Heat Sexy:

Harry Belafonte • Rita Moreno

Miami Heat Sexy:

Pat Riley

Daytime Sexy:

Deirdre Hall • Regis Philbin

Prime-Time Sexy:

Candice Bergen • Peter Jennings • Phylicia Rashad

Anytime Sexy:

Julie Christie • Tom Selleck

The Right Stuff Sexy:

Chuck Yaeger

All the Right Moves Sexy:

Mikhail Baryshnikov • Peggy Fleming • Tina Turner

Sexy in Boots:

Naomi Judd • Barbara Mandrell • Dolly Parton

Sexy in Suits:

Donna Karan • Ralph Lauren • Louis Rukeyser

Sexy Divas:

Kathleen Battle • Lena Horne

Sexy Dishes:

Jacques Pepin • Bernadette Peters

Sexy Sans Hair:

Sean Connery • Patrick Stewart

Sexy Bosses:

Sherry Lansing • Bruce Springstein

Vintage Sexy:

Lauren Bacall • Sophia Loren • Paul Newman
Sidney Poitier

Witty Sexy:

Steve Martin

Gritty Sexy:

Debbie Harry • Don Imus

Butt-Kicking Sexy:

Harrison Ford • Pam Grier • Judge Judy

Shutter-Clicking Sexy:

Kadekai Lipton • Tom Skerritt

Vote-Getting Sexy:

Sen. John Warner (R-VA) • Rep. Nancy Pelosi (D-CA)

Chart-Topping Sexy:

Quincy Jones

Age? 50 can be sexy. 60 can be sexy. 70 can be sexy. 80 can be sexy. A 1999 American Association of Retired Persons study found that senior citizens are having sex on a regular basis—a finding that "may not come as a surprise to older people," says AARP research director Constance Swank. "The younger population may be more in shock than their parents."

In a *New York Daily News* article, psychologist Joyce Brothers is quoted as saying it's about time to bury the old saws about celibate seniors. "It comes from the idea that we have a great deal of trouble thinking about our parents having sex. When Grandma marries we think she's marrying for companionship, which may be true, but she's also marrying for a continuation of her sex life." Good for Grandma.

Now what about you? To feel sexually attractive you have to feel you're looking your best. If you don't, get yourself to a mirror and do a head-to-toe inventory. By 50+ most women have found their own style in hair, makeup, and clothes. But no matter how flattering, every style needs perking up from time to time.

Start with your hair. You don't want to do anything drastic, but think about subtly altering the style. A simple reshaping might do the trick. Or changing the part. Or adding bangs. Hair that falls past the chin tends to drag the face down, so think about a shorter length. Think about color. It's not true that you can't improve on nature. If nature has given you drab gray hair, jazz it up with a blonde or silver rinse. If your hair is an uninspiring brown, think about going a shade or two lighter or adding golden highlights. If your hair is blonde, make sure it's a good shade of blonde, not too brassy, not too blah.

Makeup is next. Have you been using the same foundation or powder for years and years? It's time for a change, because your skin has changed during those years. Your foundation should be light and sheer, with just enough coverage to even out your skin tones. If you use powder, it too should be light and sheer, almost translucent. There's nothing more aging than makeup that's dry and caked and settles into every tiny wrinkle.

While you're trying new things, try a new lipstick color. The right color will brighten both your smile and your face. To define your mouth, try an anti-feathering lip pencil in a neutral shade. If you use mascara, try switching from black to the softer look of a blended brown/black shade. Avoid anything harsh or unnatural. When it comes to makeup for 50+ women, there's one simple rule: Less is more.

To really look your best, you have to take care of your skin. Even if you've been remiss in the past, it's not too late to get into a regular skin care regimen. Basic skin care involves daily cleansing and moisturizing, but don't stop there. Treat your 50+ skin to a good facial. After that, keep it (gently) exfoliated, hydrated, toned, and antioxidated. Drug store shelves are filled with products to help you do this as are cosmetic counters at department stores. Spend a little, spend a lot, but remember it's in a good cause.

As reported by *The New York Times*' Maureen Dowd, "The *Washington Post* recently ran a front page article on the remarkable boom in sales for products featuring the words 'anti-aging' or 'age-defying.' In the last six years, it says, sales of 'age-repair' potions filled with weird ingredients like tanbark oak and chardonnay grape-seed extract have grown from $325 million to $3.6 billion, and at last count there were 1,700 different anti-wrinkle creams vowing to release the luminescence trapped under those icky old dead skin cells."

Do any of these anti-aging products work? Some do, in varying degrees. Some don't. But beyond creams and elixirs and lotions and potions is the question of attitude. Instead of being "anti-aging"—in other words, against aging—be "anti-waste." Don't waste the assets you have now, whatever your age. If you have a pretty smile, make it as bright as you can. If you have a pretty face, frame it with a flattering hairstyle. If your skin is good, give it care and make it even better.

Marcia Kilgore is the owner and executive director of Bliss, the hottest, hippest spa in New York. Her beauty advice for 50+ women is right on target:

1. Stop smoking. Smoking is one of the leading causes of skin sagging and wrinkling. Besides, it stinks!

2. Stay out of the sun and wear sun protection whenever you go out. Resolve to treat the sun like a handsome heartbreaker— though you may love him, you must protect yourself.

3. Get enough sleep. Studies show that a chronic shortage of sleep leads to an inevitable buildup of under-eye bags and dark circles. Also, a good sleep cycle may actually help you lose weight. Often, women mistake exhaustion for low blood sugar. Adequate rest can keep you from crashing hard at four o'clock and desperately stuffing yourself with snacks.

4. There are incredible advances in tightening, whitening, brightening, and toning skin care. Take advantage of them.

5. Be happy. Women always look better when they are smiling. So have a glass of wine (it will give your cheeks a gorgeous flush), laugh a little, relax, and you'll start looking better immediately.

Four (and maybe all five) of Marcia Kilgore's suggestions apply equally well to men. Yes, men worry as much about their looks as women do, though they won't admit it. Here are the top four grooming suggestions that 50+ women would offer to 50+ men, if asked:

1. Invest in a good haircut. No comb-overs, please; no parts that begin over the ear.

2. If you wear eyeglasses, get new frames. Aviator-style frames are yesterday.

3. Make sure your clothes fit. If you've lost weight or gained weight, adjust your wardrobe accordingly.

4. Put a shine on your shoes and a smile on your face!

While on the subject of men and sex and "anti-aging," a warning: If a 50+ man truly wants a younger woman, there's nothing a 50+ woman can do about it. No amount of plastic surgery, no miracle serums, no diet, no gym, no spa, can turn a 50+ woman into a 30-year-old. What does this mean in real life? You're a 50+ woman and you know you're sexy. If a 50+ man needs a 30-year-old to make him feel sexy, that's his problem. And believe me, it *will be* his problem. So wish him luck and keep looking.

∞ The Conversation ∞

Strangers meeting for the first time. What will you talk about? Traffic and weather and "isn't this a nice place" will break the ice, but what then? Well, instead of getting bogged down in small talk, turn the conversation in a more interesting direction. Use your curiosity as a conversational tool. How?

A question was posed: If you could know five true things about the person you're meeting for the first time, what five things would you want to know? Here are some of the answers. Keep the list handy for future reference.

1. What do you like best about yourself?

2. What is the worst mistake you ever made and what did you learn from it?

3. What accomplishment are you most proud of?

4. What kind of relationship did you have with your parents?

5. What kind of relationship do you have with your children?

6. Why do you think your marriage failed? Why does your ex think your marriage failed?

7 . What is really the most important thing in your life?

8 . Do you believe in monogamy?

9. Who are your friends? Who are your enemies?

And there are these questions from Ann Sayre:

1. What one memory in your life would you choose to relive through eternity?

2. If you could go back in time and change something in your past, what would it be?

3. What one element above all others do you want a woman to bring to your life?

4. What excites you?

5. What makes you laugh?

Practical questions about health, finances, drug or drinking problems (and add the question of sexually transmitted diseases to the list) should be addressed at the appropriate time. But don't limit yourself to the practical. Questions that go to matters of heart and mind—questions like, "What do you like best about yourself?" "Who are your friends?" "Who are your enemies?" "What memory do want to relive through eternity?"—will lead you into an interesting and unpredictable conversation. Why talk about the weather when you can talk about what's in someone's heart?

It's often said that men won't talk about their feelings and women won't *stop* talking about their feelings. Not entirely true. Men like to talk about themselves and feelings are part of the package. Ask a man a "feelings" question in a non-threatening way (no moonlight and roses), phrase it properly ("In your opinion…" or "What do you think about…?"), and you'll get an answer. As for women—well, women do like to talk about their feelings, but women are wonderful listeners. Open up about yourself to a woman and you'll have her full attention.

The message here is simple, don't waste your first meeting, your first real conversation, on banalities. Make the conversation engaging and fun. Leave him wanting more. Leave her smiling.

∞ Five Rules for Your First Date ∞

Okay, here you are at last. You're settled in your chair, coffees or drinks have been ordered, pleasantries have been exchanged. The awkwardness of the situation hasn't quite passed yet but moment by moment you're both starting to relax. So just stay calm and remember the rules:

Rule No. 1

Believe in yourself. At 50+ you know a thing or two about life, about people, about sex, about yourself. You're more interesting than you've ever been. You have so much more to offer. Anything else about 50+? Yes! Here's some positive reinforcement:

- To Sharon Freedman, the best thing about being 50+ is that "I've stopped climbing the career ladder and just want to be the best at who and what I am now. I'm looking more to help someone else than to gain attention for myself. It's more about giving than taking. It's about wisdom—not book wisdom, life wisdom."

- To Holly Lloyd, it's "that I'm more perceptive, more patient, and more willing to take chances. I care less about what others think of me and more about what I think of me."

- To Jerry Phillips being 50+ means "I'm smarter about myself, that's one thing. The other thing is that life is less turbulent—the ups and downs are not so extreme. It's nice to have some peace. It took a long time to get there, and there's a certain joy in longevity."

- To Joanie Yellin, summing up, "At 50+, I am in control of me."

RULE NO. 2

Don't press. If you try too hard you're bound to do or say something silly. The best advice is the most obvious: Be yourself. First-date jitters are par for the course but remind yourself how well prepared you are. You checked your reflection in the mirror and liked what you saw. You have things to talk about, questions to ask. You have a clear and positive sense of who you are. If that's not enough, remember that the person you're meeting is the person you chose to meet. Now relax and find out why.

RULE NO. 3

Don't hog the conversation. You've had some fascinating experiences over the years. You know some marvelous stories. You're practically an expert on (*fill in the blanks*). Fine, but you don't have to relate all your experiences, stories, and expertise in one night or in one breath. If a conversation doesn't flow back and forth, it's a monologue.

RULE NO. 4

Don't whine. Whining is when a ballplayer earning $5 million a year and batting .140 complains about his manager. But it's also when people complain that life isn't fair (it isn't? Now *there's* a news flash). And it's also when people complain that they didn't deserve to be dumped by their exes. Don't recite your own litany of wrongs and slights. By 50+ we've all had bad and unfair things happen to us. Don't wallow.

RULE NO. 5

Don't be afraid to express an opinion. You like the person you've just met and you don't want to rock the boat. Does that mean you have to agree with everything that's said? Absolutely not. Don't be sarcastic, don't be dismissive, but do feel free to say what's on your mind. In any healthy relationship there has to be room for disagreement. If the person you've met wants a yes man or a yes woman, it's best to find that out at the start.

These days it often seems that good manners are a thing of the past. And for some people that's true. Don't be one of those people. When it comes to 50+ dating, the old rules still apply:

DON'T tell dirty jokes. In this culture of gross-out movies and anything-goes TV, it may be hard to believe that there are still some people who don't like dirty jokes. Well, there are. So never tell an off-color story unless and until you know it will be appreciated. Know your audience.

DON'T tell racist, ethnic, or sexist jokes. They make most people uncomfortable, and rightly so. Whether they're merely annoying or truly offensive, they have no place in adult conversation. If they're part of your repertoire, think about getting new material.

DON'T tell Viagra anecdotes. Playboy's Hugh Hefner has bragged about having Viagra parties, but this is not an approach to take with a woman you've just met. No matter how much success you've had with this pill, keep it to yourself until the proper time. At 50+ you should be able to gauge the proper time.

DON'T lace your conversation with four-letter words. Even though it may seem hip, even though it may seem very thirty-something-ish to use the "F" word and its cousins in every other sentence, don't do it. Here again you have to know your audience. Until you do, watch your language.

DON'T assume that a good first date will be capped off with sex. You both enjoyed the date. You talked and laughed and discovered that you had all sorts of things in common. You both felt "the click." Does that mean you automatically head off to bed together? To each their own, but remember that this a choice to be made by two people, not just you. If it doesn't happen the first time, there will be other times. Don't be grouchy about it.

One last note on the subject of The Big Moment. If anything makes you uncomfortable or suspicious during your first meeting, make your apologies and leave. Nobody wants to be the source of somebody else's hurt feelings, but a tiny hurt in the beginning is much better than a bigger hurt later on.

On the other hand, if your first meeting is going well, just relax and enjoy it. Turn off the Flaw-O-Meter!

CHAPTER 11

ABOUT
RELATIONSHIPS

WE ALL KNOW HOW COMPLICATED RELATIONSHIPS are. They can be as delicate as lace yet as strong as steel. They can make us so happy. They can make us more miserable than we've ever been in our lives.

Everybody has different thoughts about relationships—how they develop, what makes them work, what makes them special. Here are some thoughts for you to ponder before you embark on a relationship of your own.

RAND ALBERS

Rand is 63, a Californian, a gardener, and a keen observer of male-female expectations. "The men I know don't often use the word 'love,' nor do they say that they're 'looking for love.' The term they use is 'finding a good relationship.' The term is rarely defined, because it's assumed that everyone knows the elements of a good relationship. I want to talk about one particular element—affirmation.

"I believe that men are programmed to become heroes. I believe it's deep in our subconscious mind and that it's part of every man's journey on earth. It starts with small children—heroes in training. It's in our schools, you see it in films, on TV: the concept that men must live a life as someone's hero is mandated by our culture.

"Few men are called to be famous heroes, known to everybody. Most are lesser heroes: they do their work and honor their responsibilities and offer support to their loved ones. They get their strength from affirmation. When a woman believes in him and wants and needs him to do the right thing, it gives him power. Often this power is just below the surface, waiting to be called upon. It's a major factor in establishing a loving relationship. If a man feels good about himself, then he has more to give and share.

"Here's an example of affirmation. You ask me about men and love, and let's say I'm able to come up with a few pearls of wisdom on the subject. Let's say you like my ideas and ask for more—in other words, you give me your approval. I give you more ideas, you offer more approval. Voila! I have been affirmed. You've nurtured a facet of my personality that is well hidden from others. I suddenly see myself differently. I'm more complete. Affirmation can be like a drug. It's addictive; you want more.

"A man of my age seeking a relationship, seeking love, would look for a woman who has the best ability to affirm his most important concerns, values, goals, etc. Who sees something in him that nobody else sees and who affirms that in him.

"That's not to leave sex out of it. Sex is a primary factor, of course. Men are very fond of their penises, that's a given, but pride and respect are fundamental to the male perspective. There's joy in sharing life's small daily triumphs, whatever they are, with the woman who affirms you."

Other thoughts from Rand Albers: "I was reading a book (*Origins of Architectural Pleasure*) recently, when it occurred to me that the four key concepts in architecture are the four key elements of a relationship. They're what people are looking for, whether they realize it or not. The four are: Refuge, Prospect, Enticement, Peril.

"I'm quoting from the book here, first on the subject of Refuge. 'One thing we need and have always needed is a place of protection. We need shelter from inanimate dangers; and we need concealment from hostile and dangerous animals. The British geographer Jay Appleton has called this place of concealment and protection the Refuge.'

"Well, a good relationship gives us Refuge. A good relationship is the place we can go when all the bad things are happening. It protects us.

"Here's the book on the subject of Prospect. 'We also need access to a place that offers open views over long distances and is brightly lit, both to present a clear image of the landscape and to cast information-laden shadows. This more brightly lit open area of extensive views Appleton has named the Prospect.'

"Two people in a good relationship are really Co-Prospectors. They're looking out at the landscape of their world and looking into the future. In a good relationship, the landscape is more brightly lit.

"On the subject of Enticement. 'Mystery involves not the presence of new information but its promise. Mystery embodies the attraction of the bend in the road, the view partially obscured by foliage, the temptation to follow the path just a little farther. Mystery arouses curiosity. What it evokes is not a blank state of mind but a mind focused on a variety of possibilities, on what might be coming next.'

"We all want to be enticed in one way or another. We want to be drawn to something and someone. Enticement is seduction. In a good relationship, there is the feeling of seduction.

"And on the subject of Peril. 'A postcard popular in the English Lake District shows two people atop the pinnacle known as the Napes Needle. Why is this postcard popular? Why are the people there? There is no reason to suppose any practical purpose to either the postcard or the perch, nor any reason to imagine that either postcard-buyers or climbers have been co-erced. So there must be something pleasurable in all this for all parties. But what is it that is pleasurable? The prospect is ex-traordinary; no doubt of that. But the setting is obviously fraught with extreme danger; one slip and life is over. And we know that that is part of the point, that what the climbers and the postcard-buyers, too, have sought and presumably are enjoying is the thrill of the place—and the word "thrill" is the key. It is a para-doxical word; it involves two emotions, fear and pleasure, that are normally mutually exclusive. In this setting and all voluntar-ily experienced settings that carry a similar component of dan-ger, thrill is the emotion we seek and enjoy.'

"Okay, nobody wants to fall off a mountain, nobody wants to take one slip and die. But peril also means risk and if there's a small feeling of risk—however you want to define it for your-self—there's a feeling of excitement. If you don't always know what to expect, if the woman in your life is someone who sur-prises you, that's risky and exciting. It's a thrill. It's sexy.

"So I think those are the four elements of a good relationship: Refuge, Prospect, Enticement, Peril. And I'll add a fifth ele-ment: Affirmation. As in, "I'm great because a wonderful woman says I'm great!"

A thoughtful observer considerably younger than 50+, Scott lives in New York City. He works as a promotion director and is also a singer/songwriter who has recorded several albums of his own material. "When a young person falls in love there's an innocence and giddiness that is pure and usually unattainable in later years. Mature love is more practical. But there's a great benefit to mature love: Each person has a better sense of himself or herself and is thus more apt to be a better mate. On rare occasions you'll witness mature love that combines all the idealism and purity of youth with all the reality of age.

"I'm not sure what the ingredients are, but I think you would start with two people who are happy alone—not needy for companionship. Two people who could live alone and still explore life with the same energy. Then you would need two people who have a positive outlook on life. If you live long enough you have events to harp on and keep you grounded in sadness. But there are those who can accept the past and still embrace the present and future with vitality.

"I think 'true love' is psychosomatic. Those who don't believe in it can never have it. You can usually tell these people right away. They're worn down.

"There are three types of people: Those who believe with complete conviction in the potential for pure love; those who think it's a big, sappy hoax; and those stuck somewhere in-between. The beautiful relationships I've witnessed generally paired two people from the first group. It's sad to see someone from the first group wasting their time with someone from the second group (a doubter). Really, the doubters deserve each other. People should ask themselves which group they are part of and which group they want to be part of.

"Something I find interesting is 'What is romance?' So many men rely on trite acts like buying flowers—which isn't to say that can't work, but what is the formula for a brilliant romantic act? I think another benefit of mature love—and maybe also the key to romance—is being able to truly understand your partner and then doing something that proves it. It could be the slightest gesture or a huge, planned moment. It should have significance. It should matter."

Sharon G. Nathan, Ph.D.

Sharon is a psychologist at the New York Presbyterian Hospital and also has a private practice in Manhattan. "I think it represents tremendous progress just to be able to talk about issues in dating and relationships after 50. When I was thirty in the 1970s and separating from my husband, I received warnings like this: 'Don't do it, Sharon. There are a lot of lonely thirty-year-old women out there.' Thirty was over the hill! Just imagine what a soon-to-be-single fifty-year-old would have heard.

"By the 1980s, thirty had become an acceptable age to still be dating. The concern moved to those in their forties, especially with all the publicity given to a Yale study that concluded that a never-married woman in her forties was more likely to be struck by lightning than to wed. So persuasive was this obviously ridiculous generalization (I know more women who wed after forty than I do women who were hit by lightning, and I'll bet you do, too) that I recall a woman in her early forties telling me that if she got divorced, she would have no chance of ever finding another partner—saying this despite the fact that her own sister, mother, and even grandmother had all re-wed after forty.

"These days I am actually more struck by the similarities, rather than the differences, of dating and relationships across a wide span of ages. While some of the criteria for being a desirable partner change with age (romance is never an equal opportunity employer), many remain the same: warmth, openness, a sense of humor, zest, being a good listener. These qualities play well at any age.

"I would venture that a person's attitude toward dating is a fairly indicative characteristic of that person. Although I have no hard evidence, my guess would be that people who see dating as an opportunity to meet new people and have new experiences—rather than as an occasion for judging and being judged—are not only more successful at finding partners and relationships, but also have a better time along the way."

LEWIS HOWARD

Lewis is a 70-year-old illustrator who lives in New England. "At 50+, 60+, 70+, friendship in a relationship becomes more important. You need to feel that you can depend on the other person to be supportive and to care about you as you are—the real you, warts and all. If you have all that—and you have good sex—you have everything."

JOANN MCCAULEY-BRENNER

JoAnn is a 40-year-old student at Marylhurst University in Oregon. She's the wife of Joel, the mother of Julia, Joseph, and Sam. "I believe that long before we are born we are floating in the cosmos whole. We are whole because we are with our soul mates. Then, suddenly, mortality calls and one of us is yanked from our peaceful existence to be born. From that point on we search for our other half. The half that makes us whole. The half that makes our heart sing. The half that is our soul mate. Sometimes we find our other half and sometimes the journey takes us elsewhere.

"We should trust the journey. Once we find peace within ourselves, love will find its way to us. The cosmos knows when the time is right."

Chapter 12

Happy
Endings

Like so many other good things in life, happy endings have to be earned. Once in a while luck will jump the fence and run straight at you, but more often than not you have to make your own luck. That means you have to take a chance on yourself. Don't be timid. Don't procrastinate. Don't waver. Recognize opportunity and when one comes your way, grab it. Write your own happy ending. Maybe something on the order of…

Karen (the divorced graphic designer mentioned in a previous chapter) wanted to marry again. More than that, she wanted to fall in love. And more than that, she wanted a soul mate. This is a New York story but it could happen anywhere.

They'd shopped at the same grocery store and taken the same bus across town but they'd never met. Then she ran a Personal ad and he arrived early for a doctor's appointment...

Dan Astin had recently been divorced, formally ending his marriage after a long separation. He, too, wanted to remarry and he, too, wanted something enduring. "Soul mate" wasn't a phrase he would have used but it was a concept he kept in his thoughts. After all, what is a soul mate but a person ideally suited to you and almost perfectly in tune?

Though he didn't know it when he arrived at his doctor's office one autumn morning, he was actually just weeks away from meeting his soul mate. He'd arrived at the office twenty minutes early. What do you do when you're early and your doctor is running late? You settle into a chair and reach for a magazine.

New York Magazine was closest to hand. He picked it up and flipped through the pages, paying little attention until he came to the Personals section in the back. He had ruled out the Personals for himself, thinking he "wasn't the type," but that morning three ads caught his eye, and one in particular— Karen's ad.

Her first three ads had been failures, but because she believed in herself, and because she understood the power of the

Personals, she'd been determined not to give up. She rewrote her ad yet again, tinkering with the phrasing, subtracting and adding words, until she felt it was exactly what she wanted to say. That was the ad Dan came upon while he thought he was merely killing time. It was the ad that said: "Very pretty, stable SWF, seeking good-looking, stable, loving man, 50s, who likes to laugh, likes romance and the arts, for serious relationship. Kind heart a must. Passion for bicycling a plus."

He tore out the page. Later he replied to all three ads but it was the very pretty, stable bicyclist he hoped to hear from.

Karen got eight responses to her ad and read every one of them, but she replied only to Dan. "He sent me a lovely hand-written letter. That meant something special to me. He talked about himself honestly but not so seriously that it was stuffy. The last line of his letter made me smile. It touched me. It said: 'For the right woman, I will learn to love bicycling.'"

She called him. They talked "all night, about everything." They talked the next night and the next and the next. They made a date to meet the following weekend in Central Park.

"Dan is a more complicated person than I am," Karen says, "and I'm more opinionated than he is, yet we both knew instantly that we were right for each other. I think we fell in love the first moment we met and it just got better and better as time went on." What would have happened if Dan had been late for his doctor's appointment that morning? What would have happened if Karen had given up after three unsuccessful ads? We'll never know. Karen and Dan were married four years ago. They share their laughter and savor their romance. They bicycle everywhere together, soul mates on wheels. As of this writing, they are living happily ever after.

BOBBI LOW AND BEAU BILLEAUDEAUX

It started with an Instant Message—"Hi, how would you like to meet my mom?" The sender of the message was the previously mentioned JoAnn McCauley-Brenner of Oregon. The recipient was Beau Billeaudeaux, 58 at the time, and living then in Southern California.

"I often visit online investment chat rooms, looking for ideas," JoAnn explains. That's where I came across Beau. I checked his profile and liked it. It said, in part: 'Hobbies, travel, gardening, biking, hiking, camping, gourmet cooking, investing. Occupation: Bon vivant. Love to live my Cajun heritage…fish 'n' crabs and oysters too.'

"Even though he was GU (geographically undesirable)—Mom lived in Washington and Beau lived in California—I decided to send him an IM anyway. I'm a true matchmaker at heart!"

Beau picks up the story: "1997 was an incredible year. I'd left the company I'd worked for, planning to pursue less structured endeavors. With that done and pleasantly behind me, I decided to take time off and play a few hands of 'this is my life solitaire.' A strong sense of satisfaction with a spirit of adventure began to manifest itself as I sketched my new game plan. I traveled a little, met folks, laughed, conversed, and began to feel a genuine revitalization.

"If you're open to it, fate can deal a pretty good hand. Mine was dealt in April of that year as I was on the computer attempting to amass a fortune, or at least enough to shop

Goodwill! Let me back up. I have enjoyed investing and trading through the direct online feature of the Internet. At the same time, I often drop in on the Investment Chat Room on AOL. Most members have entered their profiles, which in turn may be accessed at the touch of a button. I entered the requested information while taking the liberty of highlighting some of my virtues. It was during one of these chat room sessions that I received the IM from JoAnn. Keep in mind the message was sent without the knowledge of her mom, Bobbi, who was in Europe.

"The timing was right. Maybe the day before or the day after I would have disregarded JoAnn's message. But *that* day I was ready. I figured I could do little or no harm in finding out more about 'mom,' and responded to JoAnn's question with a Yes. JoAnn and I proceeded to communicate via computer and, ultimately, the telephone, where I gathered up enough information to rationalize my action plan. Simply stated, I wanted to meet 'mom.'

"Her name was Bobbi Low. She was in the process of selling her catering business in Portland, and in the final stages of building a delightful little 'chalet' on Puget Sound's Hood Canal. When Bobbi returned from Europe, we were introduced by phone and agreed to exchange letters and pictures. After a few weeks, I suggested I pay her a visit and she agreed.

"My son Andre and his wife Kristen live in Seattle and that presented me with a base of operations, moral support—and more importantly, a retreat and hideaway should the rendezvous backfire! I flew to Seattle in May and Andre and Kristen spent a couple of days grooming and schooling me for the 'Meet Mom' high noon showdown. Armed with roses, and given the keys to a well-used Volkswagen Rabbit, I fled Seattle and headed west toward the Olympic Mountains via ferry boat, forest-lined mountain roads, and flowered countryside. Destination: Hood Canal.

"The hour and forty-five minute trek was an emotional blend of reflection, visions, and hope, with a generous portion of anxiety thrown in. As I approached Nevergiveup Road (yes, Nevergiveup Road), I finalized my post-introductory move, which would erase any doubt of my mission's success within seconds.

"When I got to Nevergiveup, I stepped out of the car and with all the poise I could muster said 'Are you Bobbi?' She responded 'You must be Beau,' whereupon I seized the moment and planted a 'proud to be French' kiss on her stunned lips! My move was indeed pivotal, and looking back on that wonderful moment we agree *it* worked!

"That was the beginning for us. I had planned to stay for the day; I wound up staying 2 1/2 weeks. I changed my plane reservations so often the reservations people recognized my voice when I called. Bobbi and I had great times. We went on picnics, on boat rides, to garage sales and junk stores. We gardened and went to dinner parties and played Scrabble together. Bobbi seduced me with great food. I seduced her with great stories.

"I decided to sell my house in California and move to Puget Sound to start our new life. We set a wedding date for the following spring, but instead we were married in February. We'd gone to Reno to be witnesses at the wedding of our Nevergiveup Road friends Gloria and Roger (he's 78, she's 65) and they convinced us to move up our wedding date and join them in their ceremony. We did. Later, a blizzard stranded the happy honeymooners in a town called Weed!

"We discussed a prenup, but felt we did not need or want 'materialistic' overtones or conditions to our relationship. Our estates were in the same relatively small ball park, therefore allowing us the opportunity to combine and build upon. The kids and grandkids are covered in our wills. We've purchased a lovely home site bordering the Olympic National Forest with a view that is drunkenly spectacular!

"The book *Dying Broke* has serious and special meaning to us. We plan to enjoy to the max, via hobbies, travel, people, foods, etc. Ideally, as the book says, 'May the check to the undertaker…bounce. *Go out broke!*'

"At this stage we have experienced so much—death, divorce, euphoria, depression—that somehow a game plan emerges. A game plan which for us is to share the now and expand into the future with gusto. I never knew life could be such fun. Bobbi is three years younger than I am, the oldest woman I ever dated and the *best*. If we have a motto it's 'Let The Good Times Roll!' "

ERICA MANFRED AND IRA

"Like all writers, I loved the Personals," Erica recalls. "I even won an award for Ad of the Week in the *Village Voice*." Eventually she won more than that—"A whimsical, quirky relationship" that led to a happy and satisfying marriage.

"I wasn't thinking about marriage when I used the Personals. I was interested in a steady relationship but marriage wasn't part of my plan at that point. I was living in Manhattan then and just having a good time. I met several nice men through my ads. I was together with one of them for more than a year.

"When I met Ira, I never thought it would work out. We didn't like each other at all. He was younger than I, he looked like Ratso Rizzo, he didn't have a job, and he was very shy. I was overweight. Neither of us was what the other had in mind. But I guess we were both a little desperate, so we started hanging out together. There's something to be said for desperation. It kept us going long enough to get to know each other. As a matter of fact I later wrote an article for *Cosmo* called 'In Defense of Desperation.'

"Anyway, what I thought would be just a fling evolved into a relationship. We did stop seeing each other for a while. But then I called him one night—one of those two o'clock in the morning calls—and a couple of weeks after that he showed up on my doorstep; he'd had a problem at his apartment and needed a place to stay. It was supposed to be temporary. 'Temporary' lasted four years.

"The relationship just grew. There was no 'thunderbolt' moment. Actually, I think thunderbolts are for teenagers. Thunderbolts can get you into trouble. With Ira it was gradual. I discovered that he was adorable and funny. He doesn't care about superficial things. He's a good man. We're a good match. We got married because it was right for us. When something's right for you, stay with it!" Erica and Ira moved upstate to Catskill, New York after their marriage. Ira is a caseworker and a cartoonist. Erica is a writer currently preparing a book for publication. At the age of 55 she's also a new mom. She and Ira, who's 41, have adopted a baby girl. Mom, Dad, and daughter are all doing fine.

Joan Dennis and Lew

Joan is a 56-year-old advertising executive who left New York after her divorce and started life anew in Maryland. She made friends in her new community and had a couple of relationships that "didn't work out. I was 'between shows,' as they say, when I decided to look at the Personals."

One of the Personal ads in a local publication devoted to the arts turned out to be *the* one for her. "Not that there was anything really that special about the ad," she says. "I think at first I just wanted to be in the right age range. But then I called the voicemail number to leave my message and the voice I heard had a strong New York accent. I couldn't help laughing—I come all the way from New York and wind up calling another exile from the city—but at the same time I wondered if it was an omen. Anyway, I left my message, exile to exile, and waited to see what would happen.

"Lew called me a few days later. We had a good conversation, several good conversations. We finally made a date to meet. I wanted to be in a comfortable, public place, and I don't go to bars. I don't remember which one of us suggested it, but we met at Barnes & Noble. I could see he was taking it seriously—he 'interviewed' me, going through his whole punch list, but in a very charming way. We laughed a lot. We clicked right from the start.

"On our first real date we went to see a local production of *South Pacific*, and after that we just kept seeing each other. Lew's older than I am; he's 70. He works part-time and he's a runner—

he does seven miles on Saturdays. I work full-time and I'm not a runner. We're from very different backgrounds as well. But we have a commonality of temperaments. I'm an assertive, take charge kind of person and Lew is, too. We're not threatened by that. We're both interested in current events and we both love the outdoors and the arts. We love being with each other, we each bring a side of ourselves that complements the other.

"We don't live together; we spend Thursday to Sunday together and the rest of the time we follow separate schedules. But we're absolutely committed to our relationship. When Lew asks me what kind of day I had, he genuinely cares about the answer. That's something I value because I didn't have it in my marriage.

"I feel a *connection* with Lew. That's what it's all about—a connection between two people. We were lucky to find that.

"My mother was only 46 when my father died. Back then there were few socially acceptable ways to meet a man. Blind dates arranged by friends were okay, but if they didn't work out, that was it. My mother never did meet anyone. She never re-married; she filled her life with her children. That was fine, but it wasn't enough. If there'd been Personal ads back then, her life might have turned out differently. She might have found someone like Lew."

JOHN AND ALICE

Bill Schreiner of AOL relates the story: "John and Alice had worked together at the same company for more than 27 years. Alice had been married for 10 of those years before divorcing her husband. John had also been married and divorced. They'd both weathered family problems and illnesses, but whatever the upheavals in their private lives they'd remained friends and colleagues at work. Then in a wave of company cutbacks, John was laid off.

"Once John was gone, Alice realized how much she missed him. She realized that for a long time she'd been interested in him as more than a friend and colleague, that she 'liked' him. When she phoned him and tried to tell him what she'd been thinking, she couldn't get the words out.

"Nothing more happened until she found herself browsing the online Personals some weeks later. One of the ads jumped right at her because it was attached to a photo of John. She gathered up her courage and e-mailed him. Her message: 'Just because we're not working together anymore, that doesn't mean we can't see each other.'

"They met for a glass of wine, their first date ever. They're still dating; they're a couple now, discovering and *re*discovering each other every day. Their prospects for the future? 'Looking good!'"

Carol is 58, an event planner in Pennsylvania. As she explains, "I was widowed eight years ago and I've been alone ever since. It's true that it's hard—impossible—to meet eligible men my age, but I'm a Wasp and I'd never think of doing anything like the Personals. It's anathema to me. That's just the way I was brought up.

"It would be nice to have a relationship but it's not a top priority anymore. I do get lonely sometimes, especially around the holidays. Or on a day like Valentine's Day. This past Valentine's Day, one of the kids in the office gave me a candy heart. It was the only Valentine's remembrance I got. I think he felt sorry for me. I felt sorry for me too."

There's no happy ending here. A candy heart is no substitute for the real thing and life is too short to waste on misplaced pride and old inhibitions. Times change. Change with them or get left behind. It's your choice.

Can you have a happy, fulfilling life without a significant other? Yes, of course. But is life better when it's shared with someone? When it's shaped by love? When it's stirred by passion? Yes, of course. So think about Carol—proud but alone and lonely—and take charge of your own future. Decide what you want and go after it.

Can you get everything you want from the Personals? Probably not, but if you do it right you will want everything you get. Happy endings come in many versions. Seek and you shall find!

AFTERWORD

Of all the thousands of Personal ads I read while researching this book, my favorite is probably the one written by a woman "looking for a man to get completely stupid over." We've all known that crazy, giddy feeling that comes with the first rush of love. Most of us would like to know it again. And why not? If I've learned anything during the writing of this book, it's that age is no barrier to anything. That part of the heart that feels love is forever young; you can be crazy about somebody at 50, you can be crazy about somebody at 80. When it's right, it's right.

So get started on your own search. Put yourself in control of your own future. You'll know you're in control when you can say:

This is who I am

This is what I want

This is how I'm going to get what I want

I offer some final words of wisdom from that wonderful character Auntie Mame, who said, "Life is a banquet, but most poor suckers are starving to death."

Don't starve. Partake.

Appendix

Following is a list of selected publications and Web sites offering Personal ads. Some of these publications use voicemail only, others request letters only, and still others offer the option of voicemail or letters. Many of these publications also make their Personals available on their Web sites. Costs and formats are subject to change. Telephone for up-to-date information.

Be sure to study and compare publications and Web sites before deciding where to place your ad.

Boston Magazine
300 Massachusetts Avenue
Boston, MA 02115
(617) 262-9700
Readership: 431,235
Female: 57%
Male: 43%
Single: 40%
Age: 45–54, 27%
                   55+, 33%
Mean Income: $114,400
Readership is described as affluent and influential, dynamic, up-scale lifestyles.

Indianapolis Monthly
1 Emmis Plaza
40 Monument Circle
Indianapolis, IN 46204
(317) 237-9288
Readership: 160,000+
Female: 59%
Male: 41%
Single: 27%
Average Age: 49
Mean Income: $144,500
Readership is described as educated and professional.

L.A. Weekly
6715 Sunset Boulevard
Los Angeles, CA 90028
(323) 465-9909
Readership: 635,8000
Female: 37%
Male: 63%
Single: 78%
Ave. Income: $58,990
Readership is described as educated and active, skews young.

Los Angeles Magazine
11100 Santa Monica Boulevard
Los Angeles, CA 90025
(310) 312-2240
Circulation: 183,373
Female: 60%
Male: 40%
Median Age: 43
Ave. Income: $161,400
Readership is described as upscale and professional.

New York Magazine
249 W. 17th St.
New York, NY 10011
(212) 463-0024
Circulation: 1.2 million
Age: 50+, 30%
Ave. Income: $131,000
Readership is described as educated, upscale, and professional.

New York Review of Books
1775 Broadway
New York, NY 10019
(212) 757-8070
Circulation: 120,000
Female: 25%
Male: 75%
Average Age: 54
Ave. Income: $115,190
Readership is described as educated, professional, and upscale.

Philadelphia Magazine
1818 Market Street
Philadelphia, PA 19103
(215) 564-7700
Circulation: 134,103
Female: 54.6%
Male: 45.4%
Single: 39.6%
Age: 45-54, 24.2%
                  55+, 33.7%
Ave. Income: $109,400
Readership is described as educated and affluent.

Pittsburgh Magazine
4802 Fifth Avenue
Pittsburgh, PA 15213
(412) 622-1360
Demographic Information Not Available

San Francisco Magazine
243 Vallejo
San Francisco, CA 94111
(415) 398-2800
Circulation: 132,194
Female: 65%
Male: 35%
Age: 45–54, 26%
                55-64, 20%
                65+, 25%
Ave. Income: $161,200
Readership is described as educated, professional, affluent.

The Village Voice
36 Cooper Square
New York, NY 10003
(212) 475-3300
Circulation: 230,919
Female: 43%
Male: 57%
Age: 25–54, 71%
Single: 78%
Median Income: $43,410
Readership is described as active and educated, also alternative lifestyle.

Washingtonian Magazine
1828 L Street
Washington, DC 20036
(202) 296-1246
Circulation: 159,701
Female: 64%
Male: 36%
Single: 36.9%
Age: 50–59, 23.5%
              60+, 29.8
Mean Income: $151,000
Readership is described as affluent, active, educated, and influential.

WEB SITES

www.love@AOL.com
www.1sttruelove.com
www.2ofakind.com
www.agelesslove.com
www.americansingles.com
www.animalpeople.com (singles who are animal lovers)
www.asinglesplace.com
www.awesome-ads.com
www.bestdate.com
www.cupidnet.com
www.datenetpersonals.com
www.dating-ads.com
www.datingclub.com
www.ecrush.com
www.flirt.com
www.friendfinder.com
www.intersingles.com
www.jdate.com (Jewish singles)
www.kiss.com
love@AOL.com (no www. prefix)
www.lovegarden.com
www.loveme.com
www.love-n-kisses.com
www.lovesearch.net
www.lovingyou.com

www.match.com

www.matchdoctor.com

www.matchmaker.com

www.matchonline.com

www.nevertoolate.net

www.one-and-only.com

www.othersingles.com

www.people2people.com

www.personalsnetwork.net

www.petloversunite. com (pet-owning singles)

www.relationshipweb.com

www.romancetheweb.com

www.sassyseniors.com

www.seniorfriendfinder.com

www.seniorsatplay.com

www.seniorscircle.com

www.seniorswingers.com

www.singlesnet.com

www.singlesonline.com

www.singlesstop.com

www.surfamatch.com

www.swoom.com

www.udate.com

www.want2connect.com

www.webmatch.com

www.webpersonals.com

To receive a current catalog from The Crossing Press
please call toll-free, 800-777-1048.
Visit our Web site: **www.crossingpress.com**